AFRICAN MAJESTY

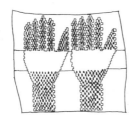

AFRICAN

PETER ADLER AND

NICHOLAS BARNARD

MAJESTY

THE TEXTILE ART OF THE
ASHANTI AND EWE

with 131 illustrations in colour

THAMES AND HUDSON

*The elderly chief weaver of Kpetoe took from drawer
after drawer the modern cloths of his weaving group
and held them up for inspection; it was obvious that
he was not proud of such work. 'It is not the skill we
lack', he said. 'It is the inspiration from the orders to
make fine cloths that we miss.'*

*This book is for the weavers of the
Ashanti and the Ewe.*

© 1992 Thames and Hudson Ltd, London

First paperback edition 1995

ISBN 0-500-27844-X

Printed and bound in Singapore by C.S. Graphics

CONTENTS

PREFACE

IN GHANA THE RESEARCH FOR THIS BOOK WAS MADE possible by the guidance and generous assistance of Ouedraogo Baba Mahama, as well as George Buzby and his family. The weavers of the Ashanti and Ewe gave freely of their time and knowledge; particular thanks must go to Benjamin Atsu Agbelengor of Kpetoe and to E. Owusu Senyah of Accra for their considered interpretations; thanks are also due to Kwasi Dame Fosu and Kwasi Owusu of Accra, and to Yaw Denteh of Kumasi.

In Germany the Bremen Mission kindly gave permission to examine and make use of their archive photographs, and Dr Wulf Lohse of the Museum für Völkerkunde, Hamburg, provided much useful information on the Ewe people.

In England Venice and Alastair Lamb were most supportive, examining the photographs and the cloths from this book with enthusiasm and helpful advice.

The illustrations in the text are derived from photographs. The original photograph for the illustration on page 48 is by Nicholas Barnard, and for the use of archive photographs we thank The Pitt Rivers Museum (page 112), The Library of Congress, Washington D.C. (page 52), The Bremen Mission (pages 26, 38, 98) and The Royal Commonwealth Society London (page 118).

All other photographs are by Ian Skelton of London; for Ian's fortitude and humour at all times, especially when climbing up and down ladders and along narrow planks of wood in the heat of a studio, we offer our thanks. Studio assistants included Peter Tizzard, Bill Chafty, Milly Donaghy and Karen Onel, and helpers included Venice Lamb, Lucy Kottler and Vanessa Ballard.

Many thanks to those who generously gave access to their cloth collections – especially the Chang Trust, Asher Eskanasy, Seymour Lazar, Pierre Loos and Judith Nash.

The text and research for this book are by Nicholas Barnard; without the support of Julia this work would not have been possible.

All the cloths illustrated were selected by Peter Adler.

INTRODUCTION

THE PATTERNING OF CLOTH BY BANDS OF DIFFERENT colours and designs is a particularly fascinating form of decoration practised by the weavers of the 'tribal' world. When colour and pattern are associated in strips or stripes, rather than combined through the formal framed composition of field and border, the creative energy of the weaver is released and flows through the cloth, so that it becomes a celebration of man's ability to manipulate his practical talents with a natural ease of expression.

Such expressive energy is clearly evident in the panoply of cloths woven by the Ashanti and Ewe tribes of West Africa. Strip-woven and striped with unparalleled success, some dazzle with lurid colours, which when seen in isolation would be offensive, yet when run together in patterned stripes create a powerful and lively effect. Others reflect a mastery of the subtlest weaving techniques, manifest in the association of varied bands of patterns. This great kingdom of colour is to be found within the borders of present-day Ghana and Togo, where a centuries-old tradition of strip-weaving has been inspired by the demands of royalty and ceremony, and the ambitious desires of the wealthy. To satisfy these requirements, the weavers of the Ewe and the Ashanti tribes have created majestic wearing cloths that combine colour and pattern with sublime results.

These strip-woven cloths are now often referred to under the collective title of 'kente'. It has been suggested that this is derived from the Fante word 'kenten', meaning basket. If so, the connection remains obscure, though may possibly relate either to the carrying of the cloths in baskets or to patterns on the baskets themselves. The more modern expression has not been used in this book; the cloths are defined by their patterns and colours in the time-honoured fashion of their Ashanti and Ewe creators.

Although they have undoubtedly been influenced in design by the trade textiles of North Africa, Arabia and India, which for centuries have been carried around and across the Sahara by coastal vessel and caravan, the strip-weaves of the Ashanti and Ewe are, nevertheless, exuberantly West African in colour and composition. Narrow strips of cotton or silk are woven on small drag looms, then cut and sewn together lengthwise to produce toga-like wraps for men and women. The finished textile is, therefore, the product of the weaver's artifice combined with the ingenuity of the craftsman's eye, in matching, or mis-matching, the strips of cloth to good effect.

The impact of these bold strips of colour is often balanced and enhanced by the woven details of motifs. Colour and motif are meaningfully combined; while colour may be used to establish a general mood, motifs provide the detail. The images of aeroplanes, anteaters, combs, hands, letters and the seemingly abstract forms that are found on many of the cloths constitute a vocabulary that conveys information to the owner and the viewer.

This is a book of colour and of pattern that will excite and challenge the onlooker. Eighty pages of colour reproductions reveal the full glory of these Ashanti and Ewe cloths. Many of the textiles are depicted in their entirety, and their patterns and motifs are examined in detail. Each cloth is described according to its origin, size, weaving technique and raw material composition, and the techniques of weaving, as well as the use of the cloths, are also discussed.

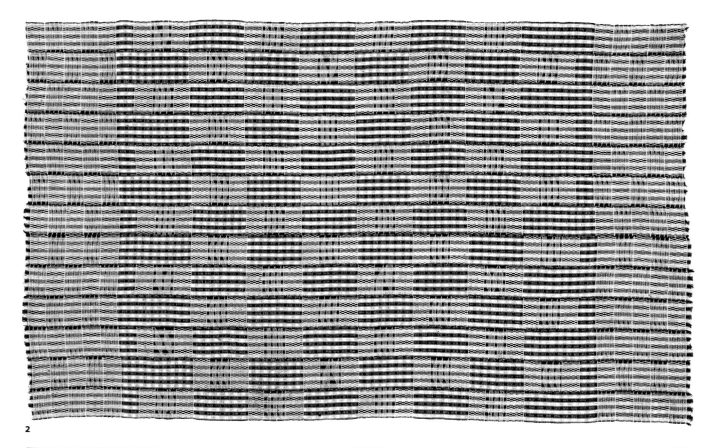

2

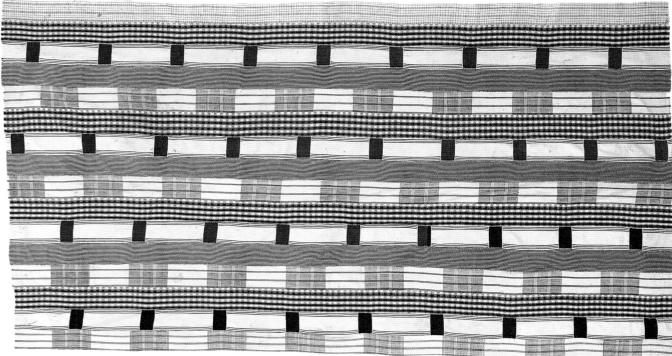

3

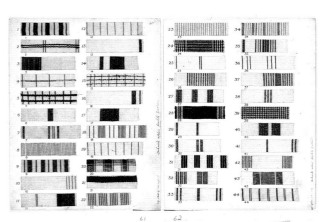

4

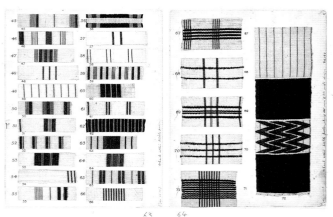

5

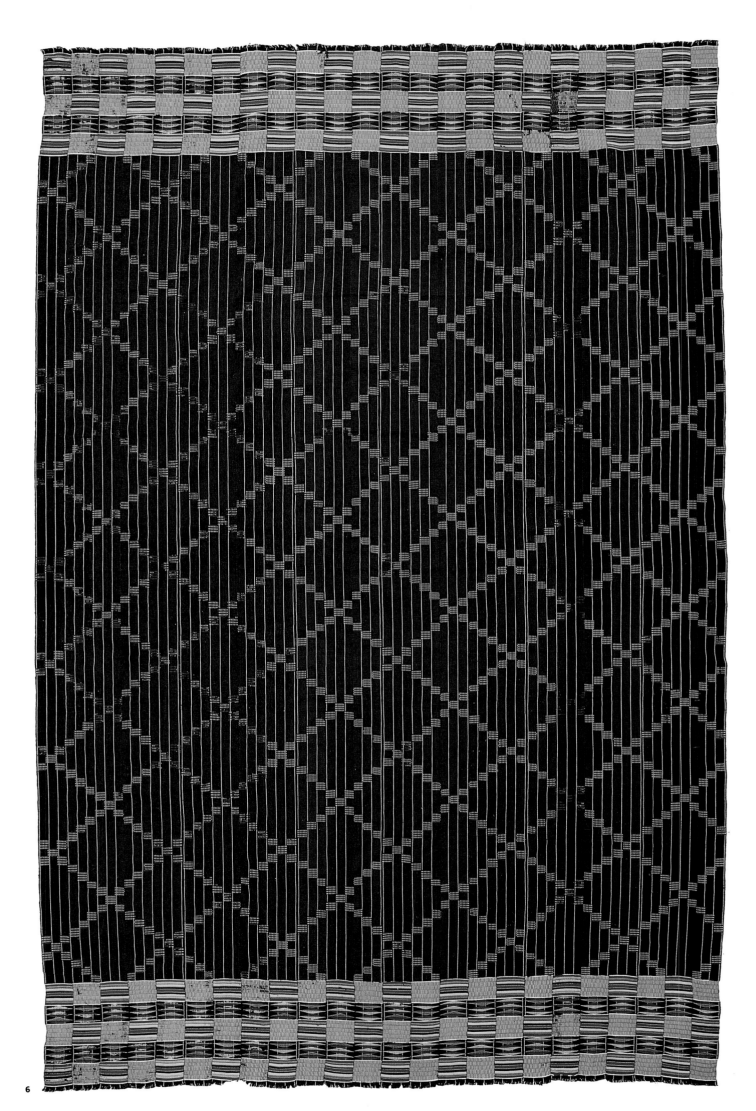

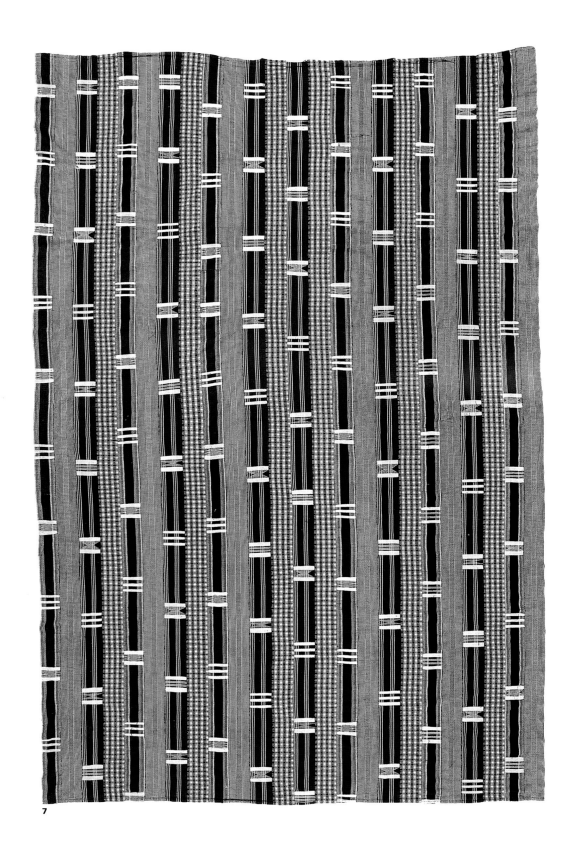

7

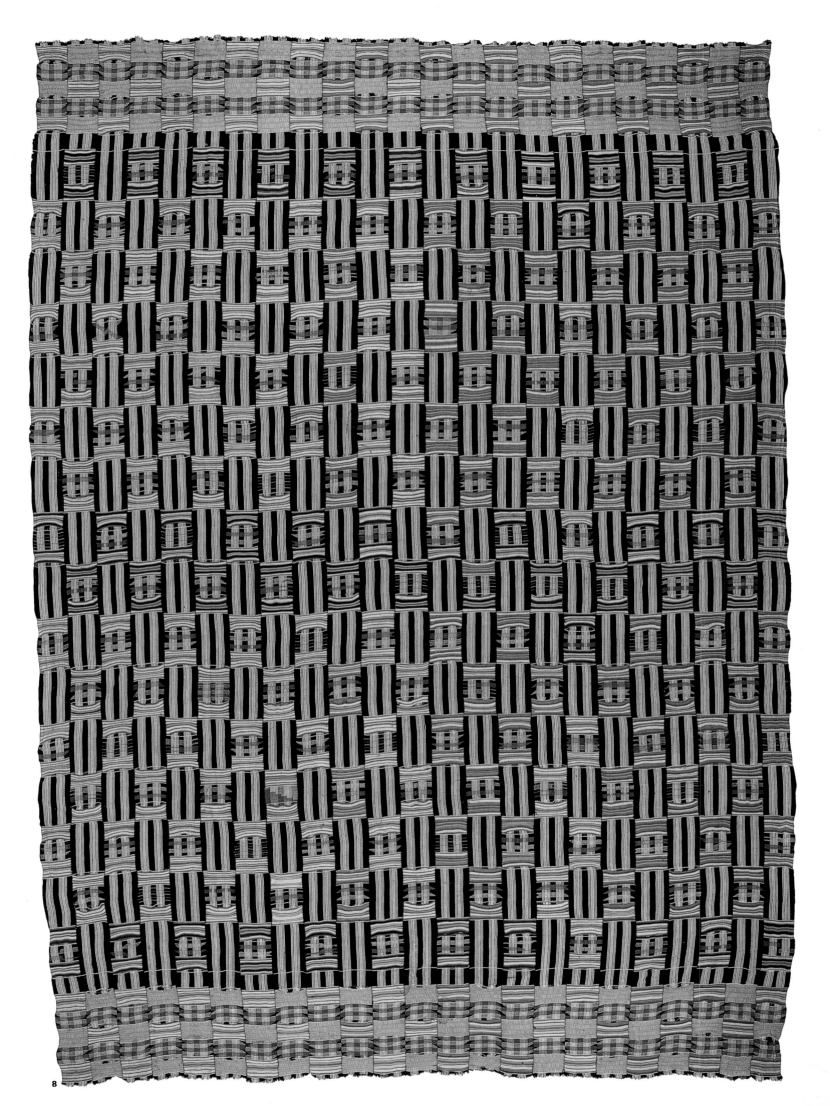

8

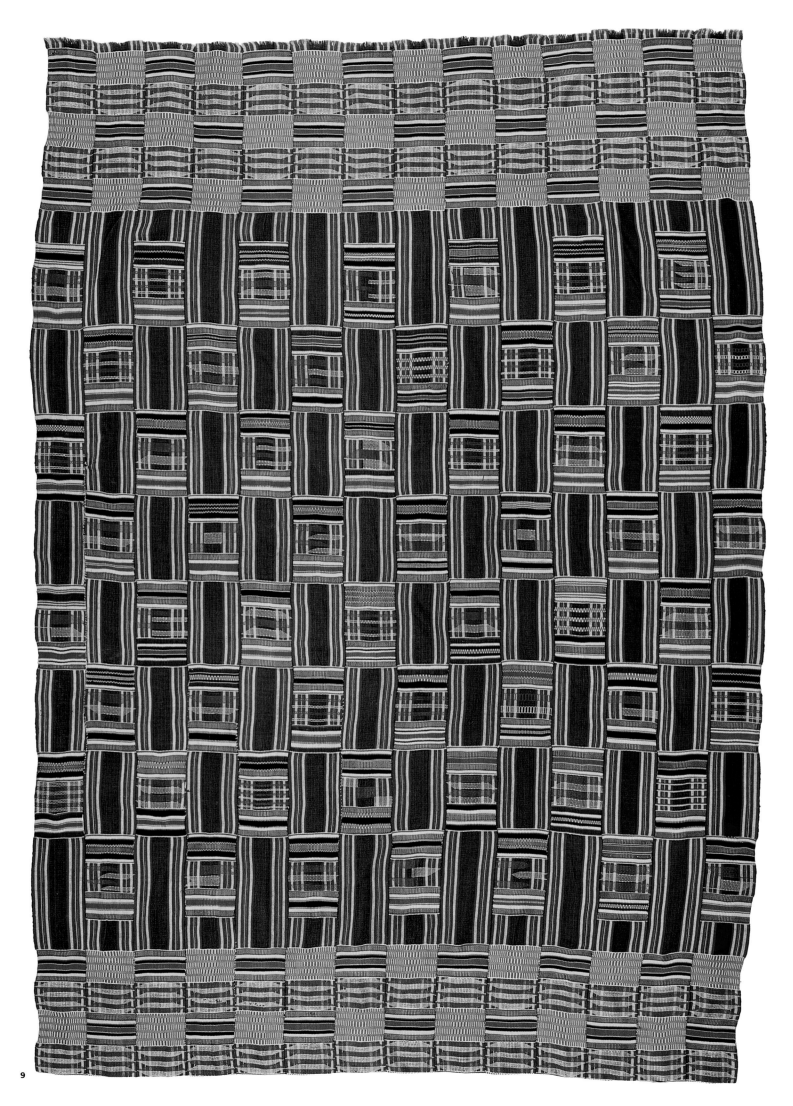

9

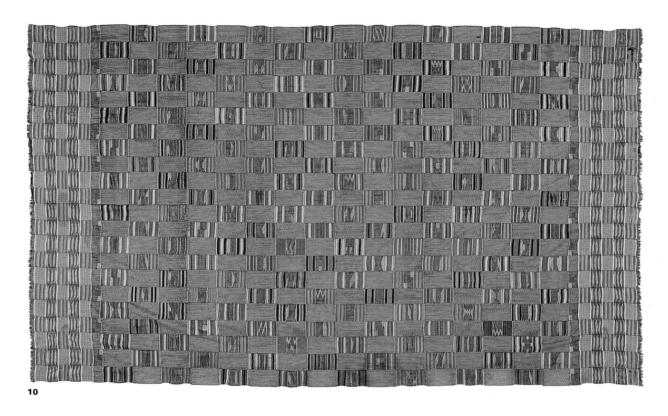

10

11

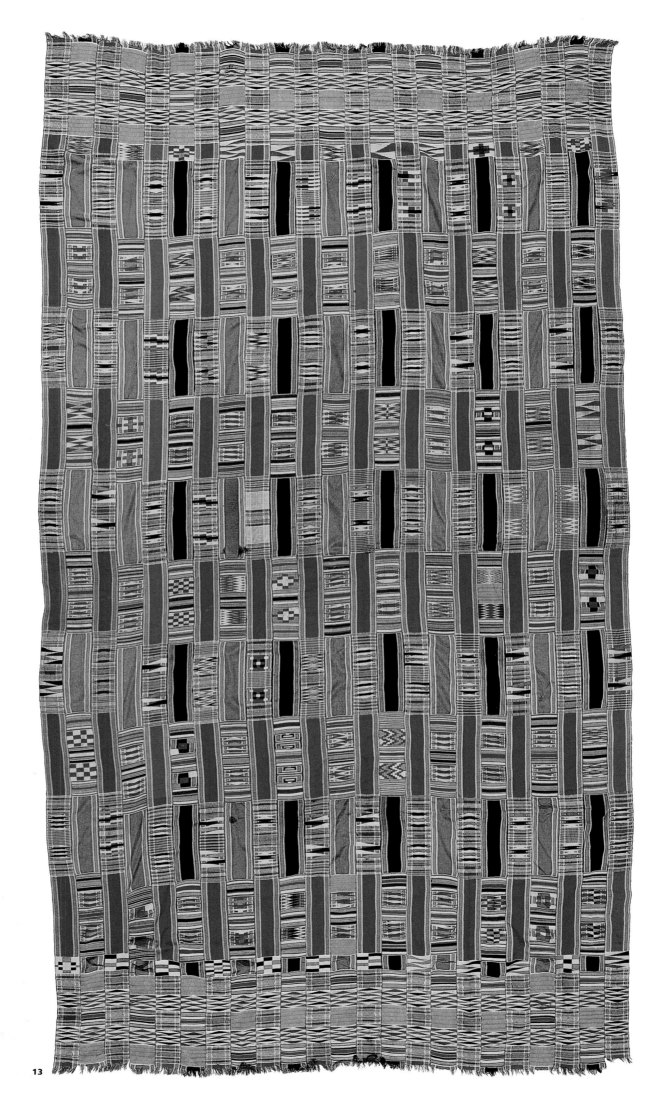

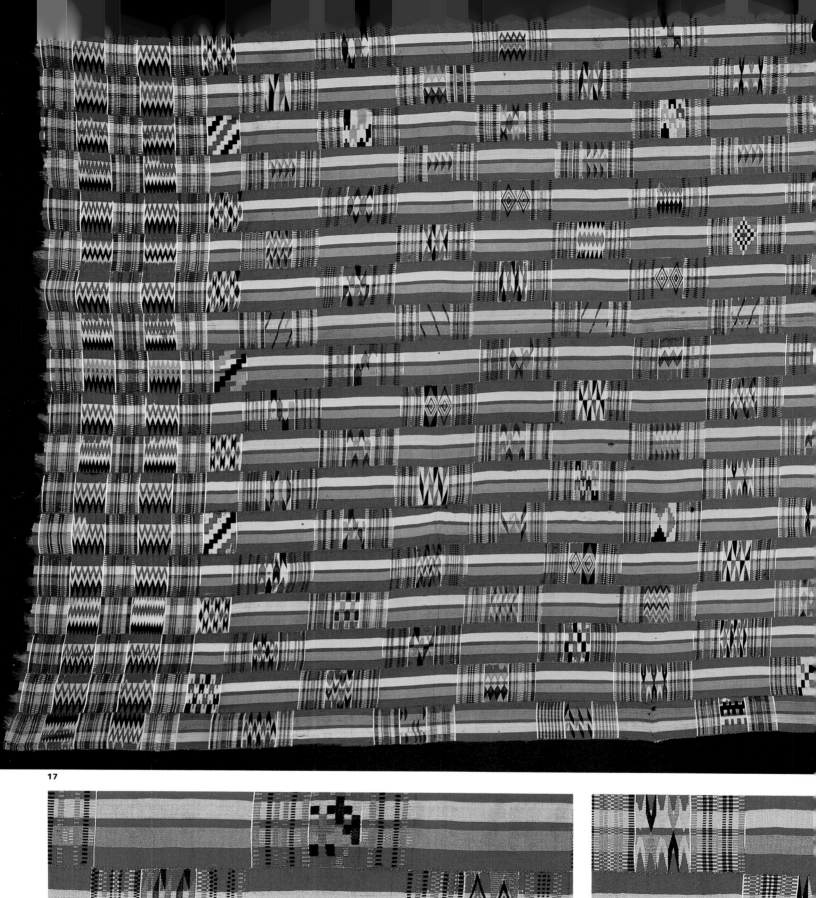

17

18

19

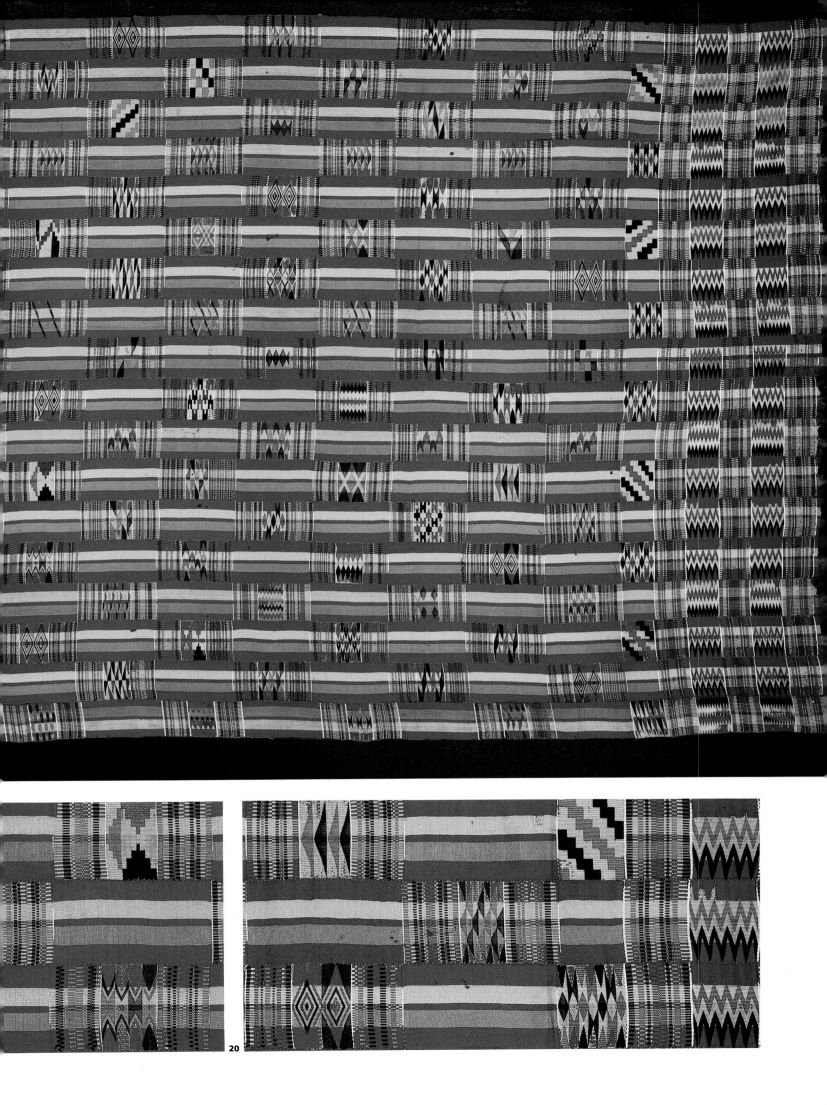

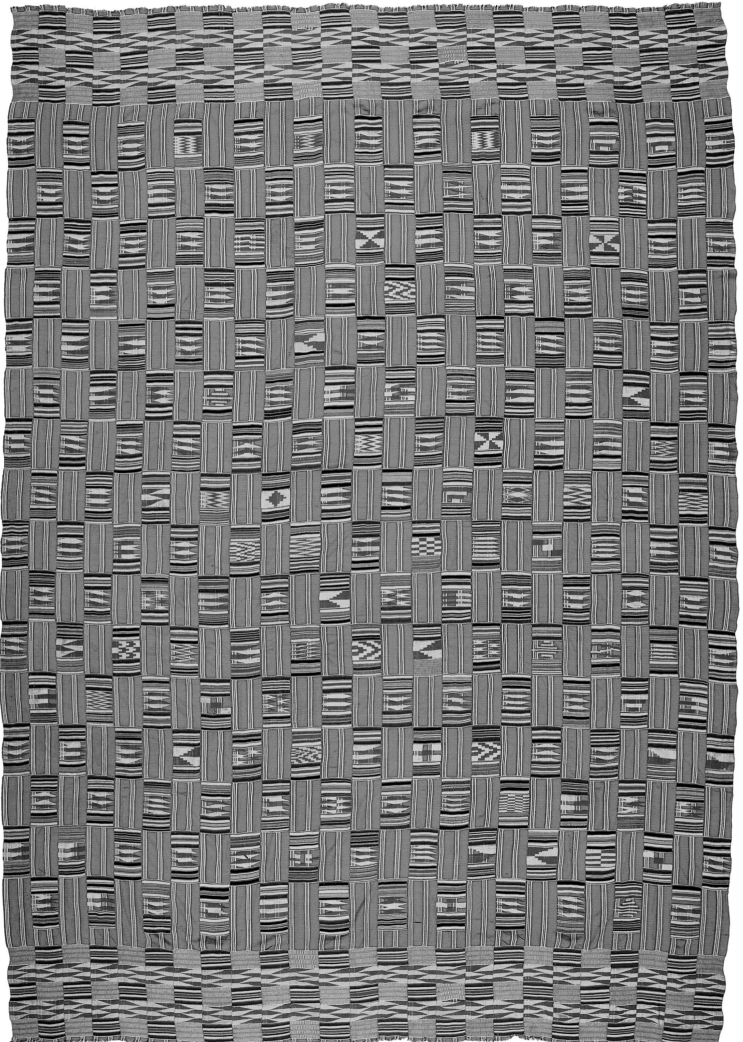

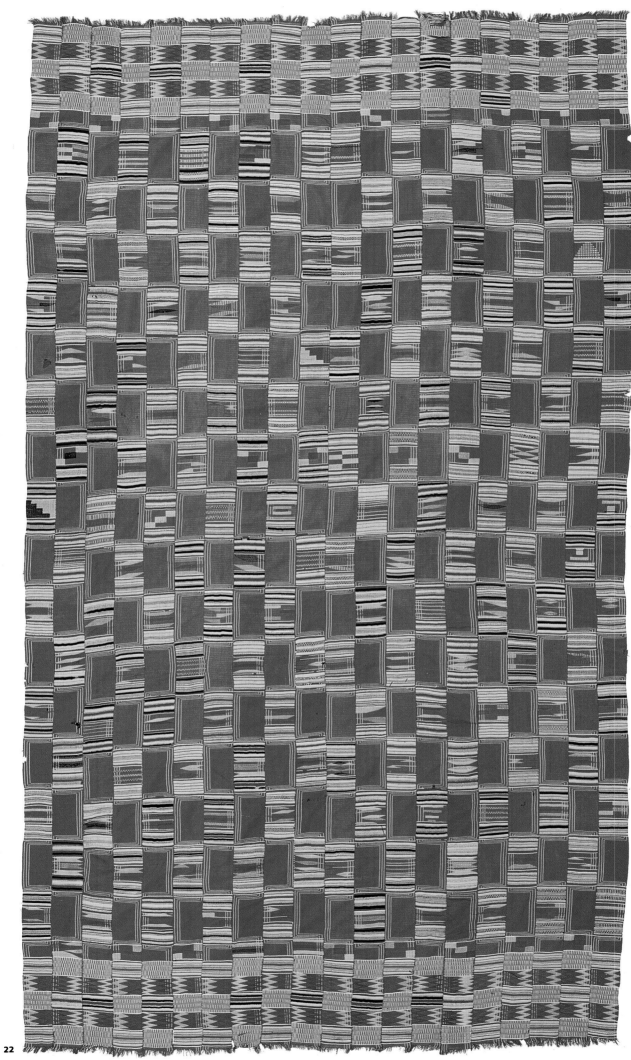

23

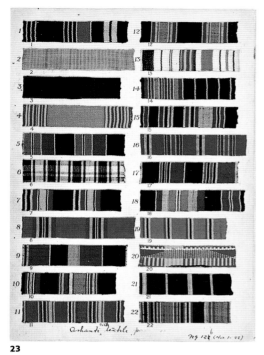

Ashanti textile p... Nᵒ 12? (Nᵒ 1-22)

24

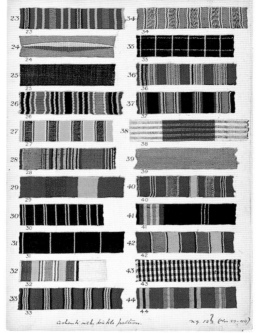

Ashanti silk textile pattern. Nᵒ 12? (Nᵒ 23-44)

25

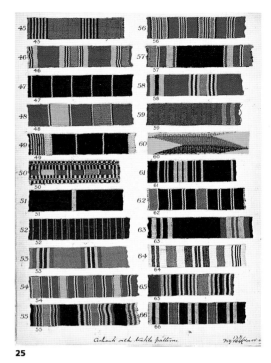

Ashanti silk textile pattern. Nᵒ 12? (Nᵒ 45-66)

26

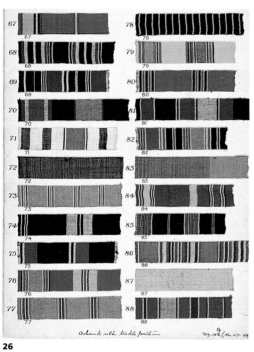

Ashanti silk textile pattern. Nᵒ 12? (Nᵒ 67-88)

27

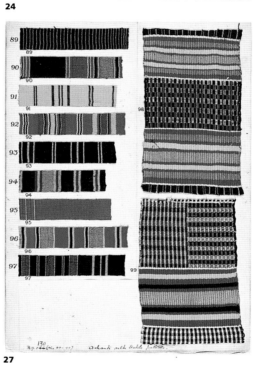

Ashanti silk textile pattern. Nᵒ 12? (Nᵒ 89-99)

28

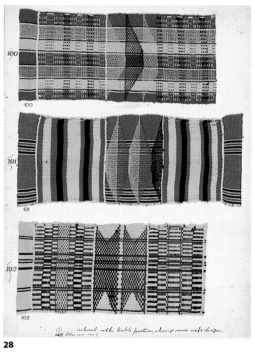

Ashanti silk textile pattern, showing some weft design. Nᵒ 12? (Nᵒ 100-102)

29

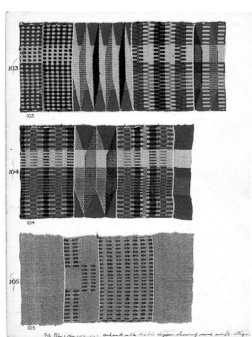

Fig 132 (Nᵒ 103-105) Ashanti silk textile pattern showing some weft design.

30

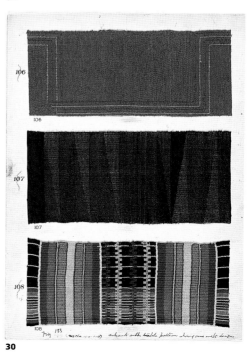

Fig 133 (Nᵒ 106-108) Ashanti silk textile pattern showing some weft design.

1

Strip-weaving in West Africa

STRIP-WEAVING IS A TEXTILE PRODUCTION TECHNIQUE whereby very small looms are used to produce long and narrow lengths of cloth, which may then be joined edge to edge to create square or rectangular covers. These textiles are used as blankets, floor rugs, animal trappings, ceremonial decoration and robes. From the Steppes of Central Asia to Caucasia, the 'Empty Quarter' and into eastern North Africa, strip-weaving has been, for over two thousand years, the domestic industry of nomadic and village families eager to take advantage of a loom that is easy to set up and to dismantle, and highly portable. The technique offers endless possibilities for variations of scale, as well as composition.

Strip-weaving enjoys various names and uses in the lands of the nomads. It is known as *ghujeri* among the Afghan Uzbeks and as *jajim* among the Shahsavan and Qashqai of Persia. These tribes strip-weave wool and sometimes silk for animal, tent and house adornments; indeed, the simple lengths of cloth are most useful as tent bands, for these woven strips are often little more than decorated ropes for binding luggage to a camel, donkey or ass, and they are essential for lashing together the staves of a *yurt*, or circular, domed tent.

Exactly how this weaving technique, which is rooted in a nomadic world from beyond the Sahara, came to be established and refined to the exciting level represented by the colourful robes of West African Ashanti and Ewe chiefs and elders can never be charted with precision. These tribes, who were steeped in a tradition of creative embellishment that included wood-carving, house and body decoration, took the technique of strip-weaving and developed its potential for the intricate and vibrant use of colour and design to create a powerful form of human expression. Among all the West African tribes who practise the technique, the Ewe and the Ashanti are the peerless masters.

The agent of introduction and the inspiration for this strip-weave production was, undoubtedly, trade. Unlike the ancient weaving traditions of the peoples of north-west India, Central Asia and coastal Peru, for which there is a relative wealth of archaeological material to guide the enquiring chronologist, evidence for the development of textile production within West Africa is non-.

existent until the eleventh century A D. By following the trading patterns to and from West Africa, however, it is possible to discern a probable range of influences on early textile production and design.

The Mediterranean empires of the Phoenicians and, subsequently, the Romans had been trading with West Africa from at least a thousand years before the birth of Christ. Known for their fine cloth production and bright dyestuffs, the Phoenicians must have bewitched the elite of West Africa with the luxury of their textiles. The Mediterranean empires, in turn, were hungry for West African gold and for all that was truly exotic, including beasts of the jungle and savannah, as well as slaves, ivory and feathers. The Carthaginian empire's great wealth was in part derived from this trans-Saharan and West African coastal trade. Their successors, the Roman empire, maintained and improved the network of oases, and the flow of trade goods from the Mediterranean and beyond increased. From as far away as India and Indonesia came colourful and colour-fast cottons, such as chintz and batik, and from the northern and eastern fringes of Africa came the strip-weave and other flat-woven woollen blankets of the Berber and the Bedouin.

Such trade must have provided a rich source of creative and technological inspiration to the peoples of sub-Saharan West Africa. The type and scale of indigenous cloth production at this early date will never be known, but the fact that the region was in contact with the Mediterranean, Asian and European 'civilizations' for an almost continuous period of three thousand years, points to a textile history of mixed origins. It is convenient to imagine that there were two major stages of influence. Initially, and until the early centuries A D, the West African peoples were in receipt of exotic cotton, linen and silk trade cloths from beyond the Sahara. These were the preserve of the wealthy; indigenous cloth production for most of the population must have been based on the 'intermediate' technology of bark cloth manufacture. The second stage of development may be charted by following the spread of domestic cotton cultivation from the Nile Valley westwards.

Wild cotton is endemic to the fringes of the Sahara and to the Indus floodplains of the Subcontinent. And although there is excellent evidence to date the production of cotton cloth in south-west Asia to between 3000 and 2500 BC, the weavers of Africa would appear to follow well behind. Our circumstantial evidence for cotton production in Africa is based on the Meroitic cloth and loom apparatus found in the Sudanese Nile Valley, and dated to between 500 BC and AD 300. Domestic cotton production and, hand in hand with this, cotton-weaving technology, spread throughout the Sudan region thereafter. It is a satisfying coincidence that such a leap in technological awareness should be matched, temporally, by an increase in the efficiency of trans-Saharan and trans-Savannah transport.

The camel was introduced into Africa from Arabia some time around the first few centuries AD. From Somalia to Sudan and into the fringes of the Niger region, the camels carried heavy loads quickly and efficiently, soon establishing a network of regular caravan routes across the Sahara. Such relatively secure convoys would not only have conveyed goods, but also attracted the passage of craftsmen, eager to seek their fortune in new lands where their skills were either as yet unknown or already in high demand for their rarity value. Meroitic iron-smelting technology is known to have spread to the Niger region from the Sudan in this way, and there is good reason to believe that textile production technology, another catalyst for social development, would have followed the same route.

Itinerant weavers need portable apparatus, and the narrow loom perfectly matches their requirements. Narrow-loom technology developed, possibly from an origin in the semi-permanent pit looms of the Indian Subcontinent, to suit local needs from Asia to Africa. As the technology was transferred, so the methods and tools were adapted to increase efficiency. With the need for portability remaining all the while a consideration of paramount importance, so the tripod looms of the Turkic, Kurdish, Bedouin and Nile Valley tribes and groups evolved. Travelling on again across the Sahara and settling at first in the Savannah belt, over the centuries it was adapted to meet the particular needs of the West African cultures, resulting in the very narrow strip drag loom. With some exceptions, it is the narrowness of their finished strip of weaving that constitutes so much of the character and individuality of the West African production.

The fact that the narrow loom remains in use today is a testament to both its successful adaptation and the natural conservatism of the West African cultures. Working under a crude outdoor shelter and often in a damp and rainy tropical climate, the weaver requires a loom that is easy to dismantle, at the very least on a daily basis. The ability to store away the work in hand, to remove it from the loom structure, is not only efficient in terms of the use of space, but ensures security and the isolation of the cloth from offensive spirits. Economic factors, too, have always had their role to play in the maintenance of this narrow-loom industry. In a culture where the concept of negative cash flow is a way of life, the ability to practise a craft that requires very little investment in tools and raw materials is a great boon. Time-in-hand to work is cheap in Africa; it is the raw materials, more often than not imported, that are expensive. The narrow-strip production of West Africa, and in particular that of the Ashanti and the Ewe, must be the most labour-intensive weaving, per square inch of produced cloth, known to man.

Once indigenous cloth production was established, the further stimulus for its development and the widespread use of narrow-strip cloth was two-fold. The rise and fall of a medieval empire and the lightning assimilation of the Islamic faith were the primary impulses. Created by virtue of the new economic wealth derived from taxing the flourishing trans-Saharan trade, the Ghana empire, established in the fifth or sixth centuries, endured for nearly a thousand years. Straddling the western routes that cross the Sahara between North and West Africa, the Ghana empire was centred on present-day Mali and Mauritania. From Ceuta on the Mediterranean coast in modern Morocco, the caravans journeyed south to the Savannah and jungle peoples of West Africa. Exacting tolls and tributes for their safe passage, the Ghana empire's leaders grew rich, developing a taste for the trappings of rank and prestige. Clothing of the highest quality was therefore in great demand. It is possible that some of this luxury market, and certainly the more everyday garments, was supplied by the Savannah weavers of the sub-Saharan lands; whatever the truth of the matter, the elitist, ritual display of textiles established an important precedent. For it is from the lands to the south of the Ghana empire that the Akan groups of present-day Ghana are derived. One of these tribes is the Ashanti. Travellers to the kingdom of Ghana in the eleventh century noted the display of rank by the type of clothing and the nature of the cloth, as well as the habit of burying chiefs in a palanquin wrapped with the finest textiles. As we shall see, such customs are prevalent to this day amongst the Ashanti and other tribes within the Akan cultural sphere of influence, such as the Ewe.

Islam came to the Savannah lands of West Africa in a pincer movement from the north and east. North Africa lay in the Muslim sphere of influence from the eighth century onwards, and the religion thus spread south along the trade routes to the sub-Sahara. The more direct route to West Africa from the Sudan created an Islamic society extending as far as the Niger river bend by the ninth century. The caravan network across the Sahara became the preserve of Muslim traders; there was, therefore, a network of like-minded dealers in consumables arriving from as far afield as Batavia and the Rann of Kutch, Medina, Damascus, Fostat (Cairo), Tunis and Ceuta, to feed the distribution centres of Kano, Timbuktu and Jenne, which in turn had direct dealings with tropical West Africa, land of gold and slaves. Add to this kaleidoscope of influences the transhumance of the *hajj*, the yearly pilgrimage to Mecca undertaken by Muslims, which carried men, their trade and their ideas to and from Arabia, and you have some notion of the complexity and richness of this cultural melting pot. Islam brought to West Africa the cloths of the Indian Subcontinent and the blankets of the Berber, both of which were major influences on indigenous textile design, as well as introducing a strict code of dress that firmly reinforced the importance of cloth production.

Direct evidence for the early production and trading of strip-woven cloths within the Savannah lands of West Africa has been found in the grave sites of the Tellem people of the Bandiagara cliffs in Mali. Now inhabited by the Dogon, this Niger river-bend site provides a rich source of woven fragments of cotton and wool dating from the eleventh century AD. Some of the examples found have been strip-woven; many show designs that match the more recent work of the Berbers of North Africa; and a few seem to hint at a more Indian influence on their patterning. There is, assuredly, a mix of imported and indigenous cloth in these finds; but the complexity and high quality of the 'local' Savannah cloth indicates a society for whom strip-weaving was already an accomplished and sophisticated art and craft.

It is more than likely that some of the woollen, and wool and cotton strip-woven textiles of the Tellem source originated from the northern bend of the Niger river. There, to this day, the nomadic Fulani people herd sheep, and a specialist caste of settled craftsmen weave the only woollen blankets of sub-Saharan West Africa. The manufacture and use of these large wool, and wool and cotton cloths, known as *khasa*, is described in some detail by Arab and Berber travellers to the region between the twelfth and fifteenth centuries. Today, as then, these textiles provide warm blankets on the surprisingly cold nights of the dry season in that locality, as well as being relatively impervious to mosquitoes. They are also useful as camel saddlecloths, and are most popular as hanging furnishings employed to shade and separate the dwelling areas.

For our story these *khasa* cloths are of more than merely anecdotal interest; the pure woollen and wool mix blankets, the insulatory properties of which are no doubt less important further south within the hot and sweaty tropical forests and coastal fringe of West Africa, nevertheless enjoy a special status amongst the Ashanti and other Akan groups. Here the *khasa* has no use as a garment but, as imported foreign cloth, it has prestige, and is thus employed for the symbolic display of status and wealth, being used, for example, as the covering of festival drums and the chief's palanquin. As we will see, the early history of the establishment of the Ashanti weaving industry is particularly sketchy, but what is certain is that they collected the strip-weaves of other West African tribes, such as the *khasa*, and must have been directly influenced by the highly prized cloths, their patterning, colour and construction, and also by the travelling weavers themselves. Certainly, the Ashanti tradition is more recent than that of their Savannah neighbours.

Other groups of the Savannah region who provided cloth to the forest-dwellers for many centuries include the Malinke and Jula. An interesting contribution is made to this somewhat Niger river-centred understanding of West African weaving from further west, in what is now Senegal and the Gambia. In 1455 the first European observer since classical times, the Venetian

Alvise da Cadamosto, compared the production of the Niger river strip-weavers with those of the Senegal river. Cadamosto describes the Niger river cloth as coarse cotton material, whereas the Senegal work from further west is noted as being fine and excellently made: 'The width of the cloth was only a hand's-breadth; they did not know how to make it wider, and were obliged to sew several pieces together to make it the required width . . .'.

From the fifteenth century onwards, foreigners from the mouth of the Mediterranean, newly equipped with the latest navigation technology and sailing in their lighter, more manoeuvrable caravels, again established a direct link with the southern lands of West Africa. These lands were known thereafter by the type of booty collected there: the infamous gold, slave and ivory coasts. The Portuguese and other European maritime powers and traders had an easy time of their adventuring by comparison with the landfarers of the late eighteenth and nineteenth centuries. Inspired by their imagination and the public accolades awarded to the first European explorers of Africa and its major rivers after their safe return from distant and hostile kingdoms, they struggled to follow the Niger and visit Timbuktu, a task that proved costly in terms of both lives and finances. Fortunately, both groups have left, in their travelogues and trading records, a smattering of information concerning indigenous textile manufacture. As ever, though, the paucity of such material provides the basis for conjecture rather than for an all-embracing analysis based on abundant and certifiable data.

The seafarers' overriding interest in commerce has left a more comprehensive set of coastal textile-trading records; the Europeans' desire and ability to venture beyond their shoreside forts and stockades was, however, limited. The first of the foreigners' fortifications was established at São Jorge da Mina in 1482, now the site of Elmina Castle in Ghana. At first this structure was no more than a secure warehouse for trade goods; indeed, many of the Europeans' transactions, undertaken to acquire their precious gold, involved the complex bartering of West African goods along the Guinea Coast, where indigenous textiles were a popular luxury consumable. From the Bight of Benin cotton cloth, known as 'Beny', was taken west to Elmina, and from the 'Quaqua', or

Ivory Coast, cotton textiles were taken east to this Gold Coast entrepôt. Slaves, leopard skins, bright beads, brass and copper bracelets and vessels were plyed along the coast in a circuit of economic and cultural activity for the sake of the ivory and the gold.

Trading accounts make it abundantly clear that the peoples of the coastal fringe of the lands now known as Ghana were avid consumers of cloth. How this relates to the inland groups who were to become the Ashanti kingdom is unclear. Certainly, the Ashanti were, with the arrival of the European traders, afforded the luxury of a supply of consumer goods from two routes: the trans-Saharan and the coastal. It is calculated that forty per cent of the trade at Elmina, from 1480 to 1540, was in textiles, and in particular a most popular foreign commodity, the North African *lamben*. These wearing blankets are not dissimilar to the Moroccan flat-woven *hanbels* of today, and as their patterning – both then and now – is of narrow stripes, the overall compositional effect is similar to that of a strip-weave in appearance. A Portuguese trader of the early sixteenth century, Duarte Pacheco Pereira, wrote in 1505 that these *lambens* were: '. . . a kind of mantle with stripes of red, green, blue and white, the stripes being two or three inches wide.' To a consumer seeking precious cloths – all of which, aside from the lowly bark cloth, were the preserve of the rich and the elite – these textiles, which were already desirable for their 'foreign' origins, would have been all the more acceptable because of their familiar patterns.

Venice Lamb, author of many books on the strip-weave culture of West Africa, suggests that the demand for these cloths along the Guinea Coast may well have been driven by the desire to dismantle the textiles, rather than to wear them. West Africa has no history at all of a successful colour-fast dyeing tradition, other than in the enthusiastic use of indigo, and so the availability of quantities of pre-dyed yarn in colours other than the habitual dun, white and blues must have seemed heaven-sent. Whether this was the beginning of the habit of unravelling the yarn from trade cloths is unknown; it would be a convenient precedent for the observed actions of the Ashanti weavers of more recent years. In the early nineteenth century, for example, T. E. Bowdich, a British emissary to the Ashanti, noted the use of one type of imported cloth that illustrates this particular practice: 'this is a highly glazed British cotton of bright red stripes with a bar of white: it is bought solely for the red stripe . . . which they weave into their own cloths, throwing away the white.'

The arrival of *lambens* on the Guinea Coast was not a new phenomenon, that is certain, and the European-dominated coastal route from North Africa and Iberia merely increased the volume and rate of trade from the north beyond the Sahara by comparison with the caravan routes. This switch to a seaborne emphasis for trade has yet to be reversed; its acceptance at that time was encouraged and made yet more profitable by the decline of the security of the overland routes, as empires struggled to hold sway over the lands from the Savannah to the shores of the Mediterranean. The Ghana empire's strength was dissipated by the early sixteenth century, having been weakened by the expansion southwards of the Islamic Almoravid Berbers since the twelfth century. These Berbers subsequently had an uneasy time fending off the Christians and the aspirant Ottoman empire for control of the North African coastlands. Trade continued across the Sahara and the Savannah axis to the Sudan, the Red Sea, northwards to Egypt and to Asia beyond, albeit at a reduced level.

The Portuguese were not in a position to maintain their coastal trading monopoly for long, and the Dutch threw the Iberians out of Elmina in 1631; in 1642 they were expelled from their last stronghold at Axim. There followed one hundred and fifty years of European intrigues, as the Dutch, French, English, Brandenberg, Swedish and Danish traders and soldiers fought and manoeuvred for a position of strength in the gold and, more profitably, the newly ascendent slave trade. By the early nineteenth century the coast belonged to the Danish, Dutch and British. As soon as the slave trade was banned, between the years 1804 and 1814, the Danish and Dutch lost the taste for their West African forays, and the British unwittingly acquired more of the components of what would become their empire.

The world of international trade as we know it today has its roots in the commercial networks established in the seventeenth and eighteenth centuries. Then, as always, exchange was based on the fact that what was mundane for some represented the exotic for others. The charting of the world and, most importantly, of the sources of exotica, which had previously been transported to Europe at great expense through the bottleneck of the Islamic world, by overland or coastal sea routes, was as complete as it needed to be. Tradestuffs crossed the world with relative ease, describing triangles of exchange and complex networks of involvement. West Africa was an integral part of this pattern. Chasing the cheapest sources of production and saving gold reserves by barter, the Dutch and British took European goods to India and exchanged them for bright, colour-fast cottons; these Gujerati or Coromandel textiles were then shipped to West Africa for the excellent profit to be realized in the acquisition of gold and, especially, slaves. So high was the West African demand for the south-east Indian textiles that they were from then on known as 'Guinea cloths'.

And so the scene is set for the rise of two world-class weaving empires, that of the Ewe and of the Ashanti. The early foundations of these traditions, which are of relatively recent origin, will only ever be partly visible to us – like an archaeological site, a little of which is exposed occasionally by the shifting sands of time. Whether or not the initial inspiration arose in the Indian Subcontinent, what is certain is that the Savannah strip-weaving traditions of West Africa are rooted in antiquity. For centuries West Africa has been fed by a complex network of trade routes from Asia and the Mediterranean, and so a diversity of creative influences from 'foreign' artifacts has been ever-present. The only limiting factors for the widespread production of woven textiles and their use at every level of society have been the absence – until relatively recently – of an indigenous production of inexpensive cotton or silken yarn, and the lack of bright, varied and colour-fast dyestuffs, which – again until recently – has tended to subdue the range of colour expression in their cloth.

In spite of these restrictions, the Ashanti and Ewe have succeeded in developing their still-evolving weaving traditions to a level of achievement unparalleled in West Africa, or, indeed, the world.

2

Ashanti and Ewe – a history

AT ABOUT THE SAME TIME AS THE WHITE MEN APPEARED on the coastline of the Gulf of Guinea, the native inhabitants of the inland forested regions of present-day Ghana were enduring a similarly important invasion by an autocratic group of foreigners from the Savannah to the north. However, whereas the Europeans tended to remain within the sanctuary of their stockades, influencing the local groups to a limited extent as they exchanged their trade goods, the villagers of the jungle were gathered together by the northerners and forged into a succession of centrally controlled empires. One of these, the Ashanti kingdom, has endured to this day.

From well before the fifteenth century, and perhaps for over three thousand years, the central forest lands of Ghana had been inhabited by the Akan group of Twi (Kwa family) speakers. In their scattered villages and hamlets within the jungle, the Akan were subsistence farmers without a centralized government. But in the fifteenth century, seeking the gold of the forest lands, traders from the Niger river bend area travelled down from the north-west, accompanied by the wealthy progeny of their ruling elite, who were soon to rule over the Akan peoples – and yet be assimilated into Akan culture. Certainly, it is from the north that the Akan acquired many of the characteristics of a strong, centralized chiefdom. Aware that these lands were the source of great mineral wealth, the ruling elite took pains to keep it for themselves, and so, to maintain the trade routes and to defend the frontiers, they established the precedent for a warrior army. The concentration of wealth and power in the hands of the elite encouraged them to emphasize their rank and prestige through the ceremonial display of cloth, jewelry, feathers and skins; it also led to the creation of a court, with all the attendant trappings of hierarchy. As the Akan states, such as Bono Manso, Akwamu, Akim, Wasaw, Twifo and Denkyira, were established in this manner, so they competed in their desire to sell their mineral wealth to traders from the north and Europeans to the south.

As we have seen, at about the time when the Portuguese were ousted by the Dutch, in the mid-seventeenth century, the network of trade routes feeding the Akan kingdoms of the forest shifted in emphasis away from the trans-Saharan routes and entrepôts of the north, towards the supply of goods from the coast. The Europeans, the new merchants of the ocean, were rapacious and ruthlessly efficient, and the Scandinavians, Dutch, English, French and Germans brought to their fortified trading houses along the Gulf of Guinea a stock of beads, trinkets, knives, tools, corals and shells, wine and luxury goods. Some idea of the nature of these European 'luxury goods' is given by the Portuguese trader Duarte Pacheco Pereira, who in 1505 wrote that: 'The merchandise exchanged for gold consists of brass bracelets, basins of the same metal, red and blue cloths, linen neither very coarse nor very fine and "lanbens", that is a kind of mantle . . . made in the city of Oran . . . and also in Tunez and other parts of Barbery.' For these North African blankets and the cheap textiles and waste silks of Europe, Egypt and eventually India was exchanged the mineral and human wealth of West Africa, and slavery soon surpassed gold-dealing as the most profitable trading venture for the Europeans.

While the Europeans squabbled, the instability of the Akan state was further kindled by the supply through trade of one of the latest examples of new technology: the musket. The empire states of Denkyira and Akwamu rapidly rose and fell to the sound of the European firearm. The trade-dominated skirmishing in the central forest zone of Ghana was eventually won in the late seventeenth century by a group of small states in the vicinity of Kumasi. By driving out the Denkyira, the Ashanti created the empire that survives to this day. They succeeded where others had failed, not only through military supremacy and adroit political and commercial manoeuvring, but also through enriching their own culture by absorbing the craft skills and customs of both their vassal groups and their trading partners. In this way their predilection for the ceremony of regal display was enhanced by the dignified characteristics of Islam and the pomp of the Europeans. Such imported influences extended from the adoption of particular design motifs, such as the amulet or talisman of the Muslims, to a more general delight in the bright colours of the clothstuffs from Europe and the Indian Subcontinent.

The establishment and development of the Ewe peoples and their culture, as we know them today, are also rooted in the transmigration of peoples. Unlike the Ashanti, however, the Ewe founded no autocratic or expansionist empire, and their history is marked by a relative disinterest on the part of the Europeans, for the Ewe lands yielded no gold and straddled no crucial trade routes, either old or new. Ewe history, which we can only reconstruct from the records of outsiders, is scant. While the Ashanti 'captured the limelight' in the region, the Ewe were quietly settling in their villages, tucked away behind the impasse of the Volta river. The Ewe established themselves in what is now the Togo and Ghana border area after a series of migrations, beginning in the sixteenth century, from the lands further east. Speaking the Ewe language of the Kwa family, these migrants trace their origins to the lands now known as Togo, Benin and Nigeria. Organized into patrilineal clans, the groups formed loosely structured, uncentralized sub-tribes; in marked contrast to the Ashanti, they could hardly be characterized as jingoists or aggrandizers of a material disposition.

Active as farmers and traders, the Ewe were also known for their strip-weaving of the simple blue-and-white patterned wearing cloths, which, as we shall see, were a feature of the whole region. The livelihood of the Ewe was centred on the produce from their lands, which included palm oil and palm kernels, and on the fruits of their labours, which allowed them to trade in locally produced textiles and captured slaves. The supremacy of the Ashanti culture in the region ensured that many aspects of the Akan culture and art were, over time, adopted by lesser groups such as the Ewe. But although a system of chieftaincy was integrated into the Ewe way of life, importantly, the ceremonial paraphernalia that was a typical feature of the Ashanti court at Kumasi was not mimicked in any way, as it seemed to be of no relevance to their lives. As a result, the Ewe artforms and culture were not dominated by the demands and strictures of an elitist group who controlled the codes of dress. This lack of centralized rule has proved crucial over the centuries in allowing for the free expression of the Ewe weavers, who work according to the demands of their individual clients, rather than following the rigid traditional codes laid down by regal precedent.

By the late seventeenth century the central forest region of present-day Ghana was ruled by the Ashanti and their paramount chief, the Asantehene. Centred in Kumasi, the Asantehene controlled a loose confederation of the Akan states and their chiefs through common allegiance to the 'Golden Stool'. The unifying symbol at the spiritual centre of this alliance was created by the partnership of the chief of Kumasi, Osei Tutu, the first leader of the Ashanti, and his imaginative and powerful priest, Okomfo Anokye. The creation of the mysterious and divine 'Golden Stool' is a fine legend encapsulating man's eternal desire for unification. W. E. F. Ward, in *The History of Ghana* (1948), describes the scene: 'One Friday a great gathering was held at Kumasi; and there Anokye brought down from the sky, with darkness and thunder, and in a thick cloud of white dust, a wooden stool adorned with gold, which floated to earth and alighted gently on Osei Tutu's knees. This stool, Anokye announced, contained the spirit of the whole Ashanti nation, and all its strength and bravery depended on the safety of the stool. To emphasize this, he caused Osei Tutu and every distinguished chief and queen mother present to give him a clipping from their nails and from their hair; all these were mixed into a paste with "medicine" and smeared on the stool, and the remainder was drunk by the contributors as a sacramental drink.'

European visitors attracted to the Ashanti kingdom from the seventeenth century found the court at Kumasi as structured and colourful as any medieval kingdom of yore. The symbols of leadership, greatness and inheritance were all in evidence, for the Ashanti had taken the wearing of cloth and jewelry to the highest level of extravagance and elitist control. Those of superior rank awarded themselves with the most elaborate cloths, which were worn in the style of a classical toga, while other textile trappings were used to decorate palenquins and umbrellas; there was gold jewelry in abundance, as well as gold-encrusted accessories of state, such as ceremonial swords, whisks and the staffs of the caboceers, chiefs and priests.

Precisely what kind of cloths these acolytes and chiefs of the Ashanti, together with the wealthy noblemen and traders of the Ewe, were sporting at the time is open to conjecture; we can only draw on the observations of the early explorers of West Africa in trying to piece together the origins of these prestigious textiles and to suggest a possible timing for the establishment of the indigenous Akan and Ewe weaving traditions.

For our first clear description of the splendour of the Ashanti court in Kumasi we may turn to an account of the 1730s by Nog the Dane. Sent by a fellow Scandinavian and business agent of the Volta region, Ludewig Ferdinand Rømer, Nog was asked by Opokuware, the Asantehene at that time, to bear witness to the magnificence of his court. The Asantehene certainly presided in luxurious splendour, as this description of the leader reveals: 'shining all over his body with gold dust, a hat with a *point d'Espagne* [lace trimming] and a white feather, several rows of aggrey [beads], around the neck, the arms, and the waist. A sash of gold brocade with taffeta underlining around the waist.' The most interesting aspect of Kumasi life that Nog noted was, however, associated with their craftwork. As patron of a wide variety of crafts, Opokuware 'then started another kind of factory. Some of his subjects were able to spin cotton, and they wove bands of it, three fingers wide. When twelve long strips were sewn together it became a "Pantjes" or sash. One strip might be white, the other one blue, or sometimes there was a red one among them. . . . Opoku bought silk taffeta and materials of all colours. The artists unravelled them' and so obtained a quantity of 'woollen and silk threads which they mixed with their cotton and got many colours.'

This account provides confirmation of the early practice of unravelling brightly coloured trade cloths and cloths of unusual content, such as silk and wool. Indeed, as the forest region is not the most suitable habitat for cotton-growing, quantities of cotton yarn or cloth would have had to have been imported to make up the shortfall from local farmers. The nearest centre of cotton farming at that time was Salaga, to the east of the Volta river. Nog seems to be describing the very dawn of Ashanti weaving – a most helpful account, would that it were accurate. What he may in fact be recording is simply the establishment of a specialist weaving group to supply the exclusive demands of the Ashanti court. As we will see, such an elitist enclave has now long been associated with the town of Bonwire, north-east of Kumasi. The oral traditions of the Ashanti themselves place the advent of their weaving tradition in the early days of the Ashanti empire. R. S. Rattray, in his seminal work *Religion and Art in Ashanti* (1927), makes the following comments on the possible origins of Ashanti weaving. 'It is not easy to state exactly when the art of weaving was first introduced into Ashanti. The Ashanti themselves state that they learned the art about the time of Oto Akenten, one of their early kings, or rather chiefs, probably in the seventeenth century. There is also a tradition that a certain man, Ota Kraban, went at that time to Gyaman [now the French Ivory Coast] and brought back with him the first loom, which he set up at Bonwere (near Coomassie) on a Friday.' Rattray goes on, however, to confuse the issue by adding: 'I feel, moreover, almost certain that the art of weaving was introduced into Ashanti from the north and not from the south, i.e. not by the sea route from Europe. The earlier fabric woven on the looms in Ashanti was undoubtedly made from cotton threads, obtained from cotton grown and spun in the country. Silk cloths were woven soon afterwards, for the tradition still survives that the woven silk (bombyx) wares of the Dutch or other early merchants on the coast were purchased only to be unravelled, in order that the thread might be rewoven into the designs which local taste and custom demanded.'

Whatever the true origins of Ashanti weaving were, both accounts by foreign visitors and the local oral tradition indicate that a memorable change occurred in the weaving traditions of the Ashanti in the seventeenth century, the impact of which is being felt today. Rather than depicting the birth of a wholly new weaving culture, seventeenth-century observations seem to indicate that textile workshops were set up by exclusive appointment to the Ashanti court. The image of this proud and auspicious era has served as a block in the traditional description of their cultural development, obscuring the earlier history of more mundane and everyday weaving activities, which may well have been associated with the production of strip-weaves in cotton, patterned with simple stripes of blue and white. The specialist or 'royal' weaving was, therefore, established to meet the demand for luxury consumables of the aspirant members of the court, and it is this work with which the Ashanti have long been associated in the European perception; the bark cloths and the simpler coloured and patterned strip-weaves that constituted the garments of the 'commoners' have been outshone by the silken sheen and vibrant colours of their masters' robes.

As the court flourished, so its new-found economic and military power would have acted as a magnet to traders of luxury goods, as well as emissaries from afar bearing exotic gifts, with which they hoped to make friends and influence those in positions of power. Court garments of strong colours would have been made of silk from India, Italy or France, carried across the Sahara by North African traders. Costumes of a European style, as well as velvets and taffeta would have been sent up from the coastal enclaves of the Dutch and English to woo the chiefs and obtain favours in the form of safe passage for slaves and the uninterrupted supply of gold. In this way, driven by the excesses of the newly aggrandized court, and inspired by a combination of their own weaving traditions, the ready supply of bright silken yarn, and the ever-changing designs of the cloths supplied by surrounding weaving groups, the Ashanti weavers began the climb to the zenith of their creative productivity.

As a less competitive neighbour, the Ewe were in awe of the Ashanti. Looking to the west, they saw the great Ashanti kingdom as 'the eye-opening lands' and the source of progress and wealth. The tales and first-hand accounts of the colourful richness of the Kumasi court must have attracted the attention of the Ewe weavers and lured many to seek their fortune in the lands of their wealthy neighbours. Like the Ashanti, the Ewe had great difficulty in fixing bright colours other than blue, and the practice of unravelling trade cloth for yarn and exotic coloured raw materials is clearly noted in the rare European accounts of the Ewe. The German merchant Paul Isert travelled through the Volta lands of the Ewe in 1785, and, in describing the weavers at work on their narrow strip looms, he emphasized their reliance on the locally sourced blue dyestuffs and the high price paid for the red cloths traded from the Europeans. Unlike the Ashanti, however, the Ewe possessed none of the mineral wealth or strategic might that would have enabled them to trade in any great quantity, or to attract tributes of exotic stuffs, such as silks and taffetas.

As for the influence of the other weaving groups of the West African region on the Ashanti new 'court' production, as well as on the commoners' industry, Rattray may well be on the right track when he relates the tale of a possible connection with the Gyaman region of the Ivory Coast. Trading between the central forest region of the Ashanti and the lands to the west, the south-west and the coast is known to have taken place since at least the fifteenth century, and there must have been contact with the weavers of the Quaqua blue-and-white striped trade cloths over that time. Looking beyond that sector, however, it is obvious that the Ashanti were surrounded by tribal groups, outside their Akan forest zone, all of whom wove such simple-patterned strip-weaves. To the north-west there were the Bondoukou cloths, from the north the Mossi weaves, out of the north-east came the robes and trousers of the Hausa, and from the east and south-east the textiles of the Ewe and Benin peoples. Most of these tribes or groups, like the Ewe, would have seen the Ashanti empire as a land of wealth and opportunity, and so, just as they do today, the entrepreneurs among the craftsmen would have rolled up their strip-weaving equipment into a compact bundle and set off to seek employment serving a wealthier clientele. It is not idle conjecture to suggest that these highly motivated peripatetic weavers may well have included many of the finest and most imaginative craftsmen of other regions, or that weavers held in high regard would have been summoned to the court of the Ashanti to enrich the quality and style of their new patrons' garments. How delighted these weavers must have been to be supplied with the rich and brightly coloured imported silks and taffetas, which were of a quality and originality hitherto unknown to them! Some impression of the complex interchange of goods, people and ideas that makes the cultural mix of West Africa ever-fluid is given by a report on the Dagombas, a group found in the Savannah border area to the north-east of the Ashanti lands. It was reported in 1744 that the Dagombas, who were under the protection of Kumasi, sent an annual tribute of four hundred cotton cloths and two hundred mixed silk and cotton textiles, as well as slaves, to their protectors within the forest zone.

A fine description of the nature of the Ashanti cloth trade and the regalia of the Kumasi court is given by T. E. Bowdich in his 1819 report, *Mission from Cape Coast Castle to Ashantee*. Sent to the Ashanti as an emissary from the British authorities, who were centred at that time in the Fante heartland at Cape Coast, Bowdich noted the prolific trade that had developed between Kumasi and the markets of Kong, Gyaman, Inta and Dagomba to the north. This was a more efficient route for trading, for any transactions with the south and the coast would have cost much gold and ivory and involved the need to deal with the arch enemies of the Ashanti: the Fante. The Ashanti were very fond of the silks from the Fezzan (Libya) because they 'were more showy'. As ever, these, like the red taffetas from Italy and France, were unravelled for the brightly dyed yarn. Other low quality silks were obtainable from northern Nigeria and the town of Egga, where wild moth (anaphe) cocoons were harvested and the cut threads spun as raw silk. White cotton of the Dagomba was used as 'fetish' cloth; here again the exotic origin of a textile ensured its use as a wrap for religious statuary.

It is certainly impossible to understand with any accuracy the many interesting and relevant links that must have existed over the last three hundred years between the Ashanti and the weaving groups that surrounded their empire, and particularly, for our purposes, between the Ewe and the Ashanti. The tales told by the Europeans are incomplete in their geographical and temporal coverage; they are often sketchy or, conversely, full of colourful rhetoric or unsubstantiated pedantry – a tendency that extends well into the twentieth century. Ironically, by the time European and American academics had the desire and wherewithal to chart the West African weaving cultures, from the mid-twentieth century onwards, the elitist and labour-intensive craft industries of the Ewe and Ashanti were already in steep decline.

The link between the Ewe and the Ashanti can only, therefore, be charted with a liberal dose of creative imagination – which is, after all, the root of the weavers' success. Until the establishment of the Ashanti empire in the seventeenth century, with their taste for imported luxury cloth, many of the indigenous strip-weaving industries of West Africa were known for their simple output of cotton or, rarely, coarse local silk, blue-and-white or plain-coloured textiles. The sophistication demanded by the courts of the Ashanti empire encouraged the development of a hierarchy of Akan and other excellent weavers, such as the Ewe, to produce cloths for the royal family and their acolytes. This dazzle of colour and silk influenced the desires of the rulers and wealthy indigens, such as merchants, of the surrounding groups in the shadow of the Ashanti kingdom. It was the most versatile weavers who were prepared to take up the challenge of the pioneering Ashanti spirit

for colour, and in this context it is the Ewe who proved to be the champions. Alongside their more everyday plain and blue-and-white cloths, they created textiles in which the 'traditional' or proven Ewe patterns and motifs were enlivened with the wonder of expensive imported colours.

The complex interplay of creative influences has been a continuous process, and the ascendant or declining fortunes of the two groups have governed the relative wealth or paucity of their weavers' output. It is certain, from eighteenth- and nineteenth-century accounts, that the splendour of chiefly attire at the indigenous festivals and receptions given to foreign dignitaries must at least have matched the impact of many a gathering today. On closer examination, however, the bright sheen of the more recently made strip-weave cloths sported at such events may be found to disguise inadequacies of technique, and the cloths of today cannot be compared with the labour-intensive standards of the past. This decline is a relatively recent, twentieth-century phenomenon, and it will become clear that this loss of quality has affected the Ewe and Ashanti weavers and their relationships with their clients in profoundly different ways.

The fear that the superlative craftsmanship of the weavers might not be maintained would never have troubled the many travellers to the region before this century. The display of finery within the Kumasi court that so impressed Bowdich had developed in the nineteenth century to a new height of luxury in comparison with earlier reports. In 1614 Samuel Graham had described the simple costume of the region: 'They have a cloth over their shoulders as a cloak which is very stately in style.' By 1819 Bowdich was moved to write: 'The caboceers, as did their superior captains and attendants, wore Ashantee cloths, of extravagant price from the costly foreign silks which had been unravelled to weave them in all the varieties of colour, as well as pattern; they were of incredible size and weight, and thrown over the shoulder exactly like the Roman toga.' So extravagant was the display of gold ornaments that the chiefs' arms had to be supported by young boys.

This description of the display of cloth and other finery to show rank and prestige portrays a familiar scene typical of many large Akan festivals to this day. The power of money is invested in these cloths, old and new, and this was just as obvious in the nineteenth century, when Bowdich noted that the Asantehene 'advertised' his financial supremacy by equipping a retinue of officials on business to an adjacent town in the fine strip-weaves, adding that all would 'be surrendered on their return . . . and forms a sort of public state wardrobe.' So the power and wealth of the supreme chief would be evident for many to admire.

By the early nineteenth century Bowdich was witnessing ways of wearing the elaborately patterned cloths which remain popular in festivals and everyday life in Ghana or Togo today. In times past, the women would wear two smaller cloths, one worn as a body skirt and the other used as a wrapper for the shoulders. Nowadays, both men and women commonly wear a single length of strip-woven cloth, and of course other types of unfitted textiles, wrapped around the body and then draped over the left shoulder. The covering of the left arm and shoulder is linked to the belief that these parts of the body are unseemly and sullied. The run of the pattern on the cloth is always arranged horizontal to the figure, and as the compositions are often linked across the strips, the effect may well be one of a colourful chequerboard.

To witness a gathering in which brightly patterned silk, rayon or cotton strip-weaves of every kind and quality are to be seen remains memorable and exciting, a feast for the senses that transports the onlooker into a colourful pre-industrial past. Processing before the jostling crowd at a durbar, the chiefs are borne head-high over their subjects, while other dignitaries and their families remain seated imperiously before the gathering, proudly displaying their valuable cloths, which create a variety of shimmering bright colours. Moreover, the loose-fitting nature of the cloths ensures that the patterns are almost constantly in motion, as the wearer moves about or as the cloths are adjusted and readjusted. It is as if the owner were preening himself, displaying his raiment to vie for attention in the midst of a crowd of peacocks. This gracefulness of expression may reach a high pitch of allure and beauty in dance, when the lithe movements of the wearer are cloaked within the shifting patterns and colours of the cloth. The elegant wearer of a fine strip-woven cloth is a majestic sight.

3

The Ashanti cloth

I
T WOULD BE AN ILLUSION TO IMAGINE THAT THE STRIP-
weaving industry and production of the Ashanti is characterized by the brightly coloured and
intensively patterned silk cloths illustrated in the colour plates that accompany this text. The
narrow-loom weavers of the Ashanti, like many of their weaving compatriots in West Africa,
produce as a standard trading commodity utilitarian cloth that is either plain or simply patterned
in checks or stripes. The exotic silk-weaving was, and remains, a small but high-profile element of
a cotton-dominated craft industry, a point ignored by many commentators, past and present.

That the Ashanti were inspired to break away from their production of 'traditional', simply
patterned cotton cloths to create a splinter group of silk weavers, centred on the village of Bonwire,
tends to suggest that the catalysts for such a profound change originated outside their culture. As
every observer of West African arts will discover, the compositional character of the Ashanti cloth
is the result of a complex interaction of influences, which rarely follow any clear sequence or
pattern of development. Between the production of blue-and-white cotton cloths on a narrow loom
with one pair of heddles, and that of multicoloured silk with complex inlays of patterns on a loom
with four heddles and more, there exists a large cooking pot of inspiration and influence, filled
from both indigenous and external sources, from which the weavers occasionally drew creative
sustenance. The following analysis therefore provides only a spoonful of understanding from a
recipe that is ever overflowing with new ingredients.

The Ashanti have always been surrounded by prolific weaving cultures, and so, by examining
the patterning of their neighbours' cloth, it is possible to discern certain relevant 'themes' of design
and technical interaction. Lamb highlights the work of several groups as being of particular
significance to the Ashanti history of strip-cloth production: the *kyekye* cloths of the Ivory Coast,
the textiles of the Mossi in Burkina Faso, and the woollen wraps of the Savannah weavers.

Cloth from the Ivory Coast, to the west of the Akan lands, has been an important trading
commodity since well before the establishment of the Ashanti kingdom. Cotton is not grown
within the forest zone, and so the demand for cloth and yarn has always had to be met from

external supplies. The consequent shortfall in the supply of wearing cloth, at an affordable price and in any quantity, from the Akan weavers must have ensured that the local demand for cloth was in part met by the import of complete textiles from the surrounding groups. Of these, the cloths from the Ivory Coast were, and still are, popular as everyday cotton wraps. 'Kyekye' means 'from afar' and refers to the soft cotton strip-weave cloth from Bondoukou and the surrounding districts, woven from locally produced yarn. The strips of the wearing cloths are woven on a loom with one pair of heddles, and patterning is confined to indigo and undyed white cotton stripes, predominantly running with the warp; the wefts are hidden, so the cloth is said to be a warp-faced plain weave. A chequerboard or fine gingham effect is achieved by balancing the blue weft with a white warp. The similarity of these textiles to the everyday blue-and-white cotton cloth of the Ashanti is clearly evident; so closely interlinked is the relationship that the Ashanti weavers of Bonwire title their own production as *kyekye*. This example gives some small idea of why confusion often arises over the pedigree of many West African strip-weaves, through the cross-cultural acceptance of cloth titles, the imitating of patterns and, most importantly, conflicting claims to being the 'original' creator of a particular weaving style by chauvinist weavers eager to enhance their own status.

The forest peoples have also been trading in Mossi cloth from well before the ascendancy of the Ashanti; this trend would have been reinforced by the tributes exacted from Dagomba and Salaga, and the trading of slaves, as discussed in Chapter 2. The Ashanti acknowledge the influence of Mossi weavers who were working as slaves, and it is known that Ashanti weavers themselves settled in and around the town of Salaga, presumably to be closer to the source of local cotton.

A very strong influence for all the weavers to the south of the Savannah has been the work of the artisans of the Niger river bend, particularly the Fulani. Their blankets of wool, and of camel's hair mixed with wool, are woven by the familiar strip-weaving process, while their compositions and designs reflect the Islamic beliefs of the makers. When they are compared with the flat-weave work of their Muslim counterparts across the Sahara, that of the Berbers of Morocco, Algeria and

Tunisia, the compositional similarities are striking. The woollen weaving from north of the Sahara is, however, woven on a broad, upright loom, and the arrangement of Berber patterns is banded, with the regularity of the bands being broken by a smattering of small geometric designs that resemble stars and lozenges. If we assume a southward path of influence, this type of detailed design work scattered within a predominantly striped composition must have been adopted by the Fulani strip-weavers, and in their turn these Fulani blankets must have impressed the Ashanti weavers. What is interesting is that, although the forest weavers predominantly weave with patterns that follow the line of the warp, the Fulani and Savannah strip-weave cloths are more often than not patterned with compositions that run across the weft, in a style that attempts to ape the weft-dominated broad-loom work of the Berber and beyond. This reflects, perhaps, the waning influence of the trans-Saharan weaves beyond the Savannah and within the fastness of the forest zone. The reach of superstition, however, is longer, and it must not be forgotten that amulets and motifs that thwart all types of evil, such as the covetous eye, which are a favourite with Muslims, are liberally scattered within their artforms. These protective symbols would have greatly impressed the followers of 'traditional' religions, such as the Ashanti, who were always happy to embrace the wizardry of other cults and religions, if it was felt some further powers of self-preservation might be obtained in the process.

As 'foreign' cloth, the woollen and hair blankets of the Fulani have a history of use as ceremonial and sacred trappings, and as bedding material and covers for the wealthy. The Ashanti royalty use the blankets in a variety of ways. A blanket known as a Bomo dresses the bed of the Asantehene; the state drums are covered with woollen cloth known as Nsa and Nsabofune, and *khasa* textiles shroud the chiefs' stools. Rattray makes two observations concerning the ceremonial importance of the Fulani cloth, both of which concern the ultimate symbol of Ashanti unity, the Golden Stool. 'The Golden Stool, the shrine and symbol of the national soul, which has cost us so much in lives and treasure, was borne by Amo upon the nape of his neck, and sheltered from the sun by the great umbrella, made of material called in Ashanti *nsa* (camel's hair and wool). This

umbrella was known throughout Ashanti as *Katamanso* (the covering of the nation).' Likewise, Rattray notes, the Golden Stool, on its rare appearances, must never directly touch the earth, but must be cushioned on an elephant's skin covered with a blanket known as Nsa. The protective qualities of these blankets, which were derived from their 'foreign' patterns and the use of particular motifs as charms, would not have been lost on the Ashanti weavers, who were eager to decorate their cloths with imagery that would appeal to their masters. The power of mimicry tends to have a trickle-down effect in close-knit craft communities, and so, where it was not the exclusive and strictly enforced preserve of royalty, the 'fashionable' patterning would be copied, appearing, perhaps in a modified form, in the cloths produced for 'lesser mortals'.

Between the simple striped cotton cloths and the complex compositions of the royal silk cloths there lies a progression of technical and creative development. At first, the cotton cloths, patterned predominantly with blue and white stripes, were decorated with inlays of solid blue or white blocks which obscured the background. Such inlays that decorate the cotton cloths are known as *bankuo*, and between the *bankuo* were often placed simple geometric patterns, such as interlocking lozenges, hour glasses or crosses, in a style very much akin to the motifs found in Fulani blankets. This use of *bankuo* may be repeated with rigorous geometric precision across the entire cloth. Alternatively, there may be an apparently haphazard array of blocks and patterns scattered across the strips; when the cloth is opened out, however, the composition is seen to be both balanced and yet full of movement to the eye.

The next stage in development involved the use of silk yarns to decorate the cotton cloths. This inlaying of yarn that was expensive and hard to come by most probably originated in the late sixteenth and early seventeenth century, as the establishment of the Ashanti empire brought wealth to the forest lands. With the arrival of silks from the mills of Italy and the workshops of India and North Africa, the weavers were freed from the limitations of patterning cloth with blue and white yarns or the reds of trade cloth, and able to select unravelled silken yarns of lighter blue, red, yellow, black and green. The newly acquired wealth and power of the royal patronage, together with the increasing complexity of the official hierarchy, inspired a revolutionary departure, for, with the increased purchasing power of their new clients to encourage them, the weavers began to construct cloths made entirely of silk. Using such fine yarn, they were able to create more detailed and infinitely more colourful inlays and patterning. These inlays of colour in silk cloths are known as *babadua*, the counterpart to the *bankuo* of the cotton cloths. Between the *babadua*, the patterning became more and more complex, playing endlessly on the positive and negative aspects of colourful and detailed geometric patterns within the narrow strip. Indeed, the qualities of fine, precise and small patterning are the hallmarks of a form of weaving that is highly intensive in terms of time, skill and creative input. It is perhaps inevitable that in the late twentieth century these hallmarks of the glorious past should be either exhausted, considered irrelevant or even dismissed as being too expensive. No matter that their culture has not recorded the old weaving patterns, for such compositions were inspired by, and created to satisfy the unique demands of an Ashanti royalty and court class within an autocratic kingdom; no such single-minded demand or coercive patronage has existed for more than seventy years.

Whatever the decline in the technical or creative qualities of their weaving, the Ashanti have always divided their work into two categories; the cotton and lesser silk cloth for the use of the more common classes is known as 'N'tama', while the silk cloths patterned for the exclusive use of royalty and their attendants are known as 'Asasia'. The Asasia cloths are an exclusive variety of the all-silk weavings and form a category in their own right. N'tama silk cloths of vivid colours and exotic patterns may be worn by nobles and merchants and caboceers; their use is of no interest to the Asantehene. It is the royal cloths and the robes of the inner circle of the court, the Asasia, that the chief of chiefs and his family commission, use and distribute with all due ceremony to their most worthy subjects in return for faithful service to the Golden Stool.

The Asasia cloths are woven in Bonwire under the careful and close supervision of the chief of the time; these textiles are commissioned as the private property of the Asantehene, and their techniques of construction and patterning are held to be a royal secret. Rattray makes no mention

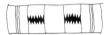

of the Asasia cloths in *Religion and Art in Ashanti* (1927), presumably because such knowledge was withheld from him, despite his high standing as a colonial intimately sympathetic to the Ashanti. Unfortunately, Rattray has also confused the issue of attribution by describing as exclusively royal many cloths that are certainly not woven using the Asasia technique.

It is indeed by their technique, as well as by their composition, that the Asasia cloths are differentiated from all other Ashanti silk strip-weaves. By increasing the number of heddles on the loom from two pairs to three pairs, the weaver may pick up a greater number of warp threads at any one time; this has the advantage of allowing greater versatility, which allows intricate patterns of inlaid twill to be inserted. It is the presence of patterns in this distinctive twill that characterizes the Asasia cloth, together with, of course, the patterns themselves, which are the exclusive preserve of these royal vestments. Owing to technical limitations, all the twill patterning must follow a diagonal path across the warp, and so the patterns form a delightful combination of zig-zags, interlocking triangles and arrow flèches. Asasia cloths, unlike all other Ashanti strip-weaves, whether of cotton or silk, are named after these exclusive patterns and their compositions, rather than the striping on the background warp.

Lamb declares that all the Asasia cloths hitherto seen have been woven with the characteristic red-, green- and yellow-striped 'Oyokoman' background. Rattray gives the full title of this type of warp striping as: '"Oyokoman ogya da mu" ("There is a fire between the two factions of the Oyoko clan"); referring to the civil war after the death of Osei Tutu between Opuku Ware and the Dako. This cloth was worn by the King of Ashanti at the Kwesi Adae (Sunday Adae ceremony). It is the clan "tartan" of the Royal House.' Of all the Ashanti weaving of silken cloths, the six-heddled Asasia production is the most complex, the most time-consuming and therefore the most costly. In contrast to the other strip-woven cloth production, it is the loss of skill and the failure to hand down knowledge of the patterns that will hasten the decline of Asasia production. The following observation by Lamb in May 1972 sounds distinctly gloomy: 'It is a tragic fact that the one remaining weaver alive in Bonwire at the time of writing who remembers the Asasia patterns is no longer capable of weaving them. A proper, full-size Asasia cloth, it is said, has not been woven since before World War II, even though, so I was told by the Bonwire Chief, the Asantehene Prempeh II, who came to the throne in 1931, used to take a considerable personal interest in cloth and even make up his own designs for Bonwire weavers to execute. But even the Asantehene's interest did not seem to have sufficed to keep the Asasia weaving tradition flourishing. After Prempeh II's death in 1970 the general opinion in Bonwire was that it would be far from easy, and perhaps impossible, to execute the kind of order traditionally made by a new Asantehene. The Bonwire Chief told me that some kind of cloth had been ordered by the new Asantehene, Opokuware II, but I was unable to learn anything about either its style or the skill with which it was being woven, though I knew there were anxieties on that last point.' The health of this elitist form of Ashanti silk-weaving has naturally reflected the changing political and economic fortunes of the Ashanti royalty: the Asasia cloth originated after the seventeenth century, production flourished in the eighteenth and nineteenth centuries and has been in severe decline in the twentieth century.

The Ashanti title for their strip-woven cloths, N'tama, refers to a general quality of cloth that is not Asasia. There is a second ranking of cloth, however, and that is 'Nsaduaso'. These are the cloths a wealthy man might commission; made of the finest silks, they contain none of the taboo techniques of twill or patterns in twill. Cloth types are further divided according to the complexity of the pattern inlays, or the lack of such inlays. Cotton or silk cloth patterned with simple warp stripes is known as 'Ahwepan'. Cloth with simple weft inlays through which the background warp stripes of the bands may be clearly seen is entitled 'Topreko'. These textiles are predominantly of silk. The finest quality silk cloth, in terms of pattern complexity, other than Asasia, is 'Faprenu'. Here, the inlays are worked using a double weave technique and are packed down so tightly that the background stripes of colour are obscured. Inlay patterns have a name that is associated with the design itself and, less frequently, with their arrangement within the overall composition. The best known example of this unusual custom is the pin-striped blue silk cloth that is thinly latticed with a regimented grid of lozenges formed of tiny rectangular inlays of yellow and maroon. This cloth is known as 'Akyempim' ('He has given him one thousand') (plate 24, no. 31). It is traditionally dated to the reign of Osei Tutu (eighteenth century) and owes its origin to a gift from that monarch to one Owusu Efiriye, the Akyempim chief. A cloth that is patterned throughout with connecting blocks of inlay patterns is the supreme achievement of the Faprenu weaver. These cloths have a supplementary title that is appropriate to the way in which they test the imagination and the endurance of the weaver. They are known as 'Adweneasa', the literal translation of which is 'My skill is exhausted' or 'My ideas have come to an end'; this refers to the lack of space on the cloth into which yet more blocks of inlay might be packed. As one might imagine, from Ahwepan to Faprenu there is a scale of increasing complexity of weaving technique, which is matched by the extra demand for silk, because of the augmented density of the inlays; this, in turn, is reflected in the increased value of the cloth.

As well as being titled according to the intensity of the inlays, as I have already mentioned, all cloths other than the Asasia are given an individual name derived from the arrangement of the warp stripes. There are over three hundred standard arrangements of warp threads in use today, and more are added from time to time to satisfy the demands of the ever-fashionable Ghanaian. The predominantly blue-and-white cotton weaves have rather inventive titles which belie their more humble status; examples include 'Hiampoa' ('I lack even a penny') (plate 4, no. 6), 'Ntontom beforo'po?'('Does a mosquito cross the sea?') (plate 5, no. 61), 'Ennamenkoso' ('The fault is not mine') (plate 5, no. 67) and 'Ademkyemyamu' ('Inside the belly of the crocodile') (plate 4, no. 24).

The background stripes of the silk cloths, as befits their expense and therefore their status, have inspired more elaborate titles. These include 'Nkwantia ogye akore' ('It is at the small crossroads that the sacrifice is pegged down') (plate 23, no. 16), 'Yaa Amanpene' ('Yaa whom the nation loves': Yaa was one of the daughters of King Osei Kojo) (plate 25, no. 55), 'Anwonomoase' ('Root of the anwonomo plant': after an Akan saying, 'The anwonomo root is sweet' – the design signifies happiness) (plate 27, no. 96), 'Nku me fie' ('My murderer should not come from my own kin'), and 'Kradie' ('The satisfied soul') (plate 27, no. 92).

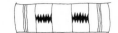

Cotton or silk cloths that have been woven of strips whose warp patterns do not match across the cloth are given the title 'Mmaban', which means mixed. Many of the older cloths of the Ashanti are decorated in this way, with the blocks of colour and pattern being 'mis-matched' across the whole cloth to create a satisfying overall effect. The result is often one of great graphic intensity, as the eye is drawn from the blocks of pattern and colours within one strip or group of strips to the adjacent bands, which provide contrast and break up the composition. Today this practice is derided as the work of a weaver eager to use up the strips left over from the construction of many different cloths, and is idly dismissed as 'mix mix'. The even and alternate spacing of the blocks of pattern and blocks of colour (*babadua*) is known as *susudua*, and occurs not only as a pattern repeat on each strip, but across the strips, creating a chequerboard effect over the whole cloth. This change of emphasis in the last forty years towards a more regimented patterning of identical strip colours and evenly spaced patterns or blocks of colour is a manifestation of the mediocre habits of modern weavers, inspired by unimaginative commissions from a society corrupted by the decadent consumerism of the Western world.

The cloths of the Ashanti continue to play a most important role in their lives, for as well as providing the colourful robes worn at ceremonial and religious events, where they are valued for their status-enhancing qualities, the patterns and designs on these cloths are appreciated for the historical anecdotes represented by their names – providing yet another connection with the Akan oral culture of the proverb, and a method by which the new fashions of the culture may be expressed. In this way there has been a fluid development of colour and pattern popularity governed by both royal and common demand.

In the past, for the senior members of Ashanti society, the use of fine cloths was governed by status, and hence wealth, as well as etiquette. Until recently it would have been unthinkable, as well as financially impossible, for a younger man of no status to order a fine silk cloth. The strict hierarchy not only separated royalty from any other members of the group through the exclusive use of Asasia cloths, but also ensured that the sporting of the lesser silk cloths was regulated by a

rigid class system. A lesser chief, let alone an ordinary man, would be at pains to ensure that his garments should by no means outshine those worn by a more senior chief at a festival. Chiefly status and wealth were inseparable, and so a durbar of these leaders was an occasion when an extravagant show of finery clearly indicated the levels of rank to the gathered populace.

This clear and immutable social order, like the level of design ingenuity in the cloths, has seemingly weakened over the past fifty years as a result of the relative diminution in power of the chiefs. However, whilst it is certain that more and more people are seen wearing fine and expensive cloths who would not have been 'eligible' to do so in the past, this is perhaps more a reflection of the general increase and spread of wealth beyond the chiefs in late twentieth-century Ghana, than an indication that the social order itself is being eroded. From the Ashanti oral traditions Lamb has noted that in times past the wealth of the individual could also buy the status of a fine cloth; any murmurings of disenchantment concerning this matter from the chiefs of today reflects, therefore, dismay at the increased numbers of expensive silk cloths on display, rather than fear of a complete breakdown of the hierarchy. What must irk them, however, is the loss of visual focus that is apparent at any meeting of chiefs and senior citizens; the wealth of dazzling silk and rayon cloths on show certainly dilutes the impact made by the chiefs and royal family, no matter how exclusive their cloths are. Such cloths are now found in use beyond the Ashanti and Ghanaian borders, further 'decentralizing' their status. The more general use of strip-woven cloth as a robe has grown in popularity from West to Central Africa since the rush to independence in the late 1950s, as it is considered to represent a 'traditional' and pan-African form of dress, as opposed to the European and 'colonial' style. Of all the strip-weaves, the brightly patterned and luxurious strip-weaves of Ashanti origin are the most highly prized by the wealthy merchants and politicians of many African states.

It is not only the richness of the silk and the complexity of the patterns in many Ashanti cloths that make an impact on the onlooker, for colour may also be used to invoke a mood. A chief will more than likely sport a cloth with much golden yellow colour, made yet more sumptuous by red and blue panels or motifs; gold and golden colours quite obviously represent wealth and joy. Lamb questioned her Bonwire informants and noted the following: '. . . a Queen Mother, or even a more humble woman, might wear silver, white or blue to signify purity, virtue or joy. White is usually worn by priestesses to symbolize deities or the spirits of the ancestors. Green may be worn by young girls to suggest newness, freshness and puberty. Black can stand for melancholy, vice, devils, old age, death and even history. Red is commonly worn for loss, sadness, death or dissatisfaction. Sometimes red is worn at political meetings to indicate anger.'

The wearing of cloths as ritual attire is evident in the Akan, as well as Ewe cultures, and the ways in which they are worn demonstrate the place of the bearer in relation to the living and the dead. Revealing the full torso is a sign of modesty and respect, and the toga-like manner in which the cloths are worn effortlessly allows for this simple movement of partial disrobing; the cloth can be slipped off the left shoulder and tucked into the waist as the supplicant greets or dances before a royal personage or senior. The same sign of humility is displayed when visiting shrines, at burial ceremonies and at other religious affairs. A further indication of respect is achieved by wearing cotton or silk Ahwepan or Topreko N'tama cloths when visiting the ancestral shrines; being unpatterned or simply patterned, and often old, these cloths are of a lesser quality, and so indicate appropriate feelings of humility.

Not only do the living respect the dead by a modest display of their cloth, but by contrast the casks and shrines of the recently deceased are honoured with a swathe of very valuable cloths. The funerals of senior Ashanti figures, and particularly the Asantehene, are an opportunity to erect a cloth-caparisoned structure around or over the litter of the body lying in state, and to decorate the bed itself with fine indigenous strip-weaves, as well as the 'foreign' cloth of the Fulani. Bowdich asserts that, in his time, such display extended to burying the dead with a wealth of cloth that emphasized their status. This practice seems to be no longer current, though strip-weave cloths are commonly used throughout West Africa to divide the area of the living from the bed of the dead within a house.

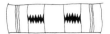

Although present-day gatherings of the Ashanti and neighbouring Akan groups are still characterized by the enthusiastic display of colourful strip-weave cloths, there is absolutely no doubt that the quality and range of Ashanti strip-weave designs, colour fields and techniques have been in decline over the past forty to sixty years. The total number of weavers, as well as the proportion of their time spent weaving in relation to other activities, is also decreasing.

As the commissioning drive of royalty and chiefs that once drove the production of fine and 'traditional' cloths has fallen into decline, so the recently renewed rise in demand for the strip-weaves has come from a less discerning consumer; at the same time, the weavers have been restricted in their ability to create the designs they would like to produce, as quality yarns have been less easy to obtain or have become prohibitively expensive. These factors have created a customer base happy to buy second-rate cloth of a limited colour and pattern range, which is supplied by weavers whose skills can no longer be tested to the full, and whose apprentices learn little of the abundance of designs and technical excellence of the recent past. These young weavers have not the time to learn of the painstaking and complex workmanship of their forebears, for there is a ready and remunerative market in easy-to-make strip-weave accessories and brash, simply patterned cloth for the tourist and export market. To be closer to this demand and to meet the needs of its ephemeral fashions, many weavers have moved to Accra and its urban hinterland.

A stroll through the cloth market in Accra illustrates the strange times that the Ashanti weavers face. At the entrance to each stall are the recently woven tourist and small consumer trappings. Their lack of workmanship and creative ingenuity is completely alien to the work of their predecessors, which drapes the walls of each cubicle. The royal and chiefly commissions have been replaced by the demands of the export and tourist merchant. No wonder, then, that very few complete new cloths of any description are seen for sale. There is tragic irony in the fact that the demand that does exist for superior cloths continues to be met from an Ashanti source – but it is from old strip-weaves preserved in the family coffers, and not from the loom. One day this stock of historic weaves will run dry. Inevitably, there will be no replacements.

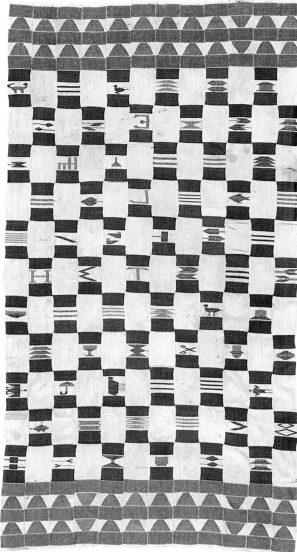

32

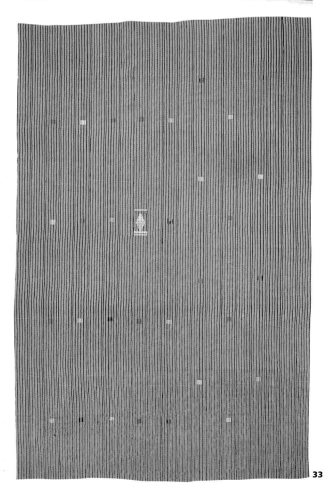

33

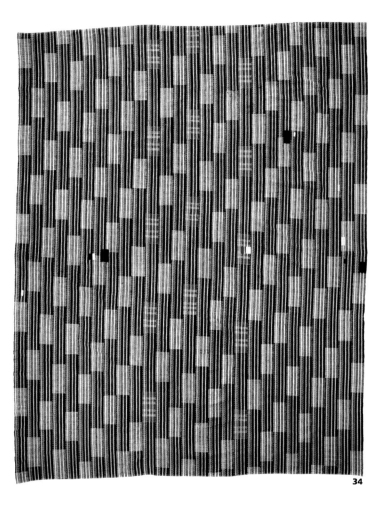

34

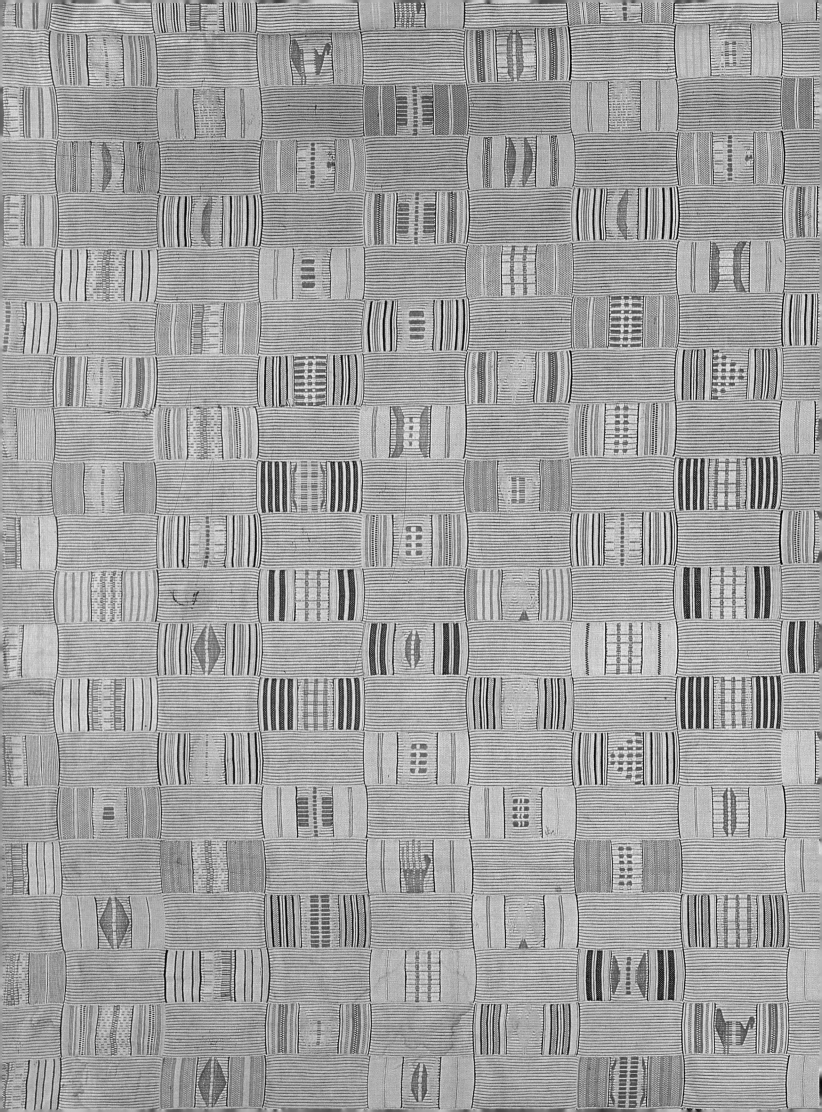

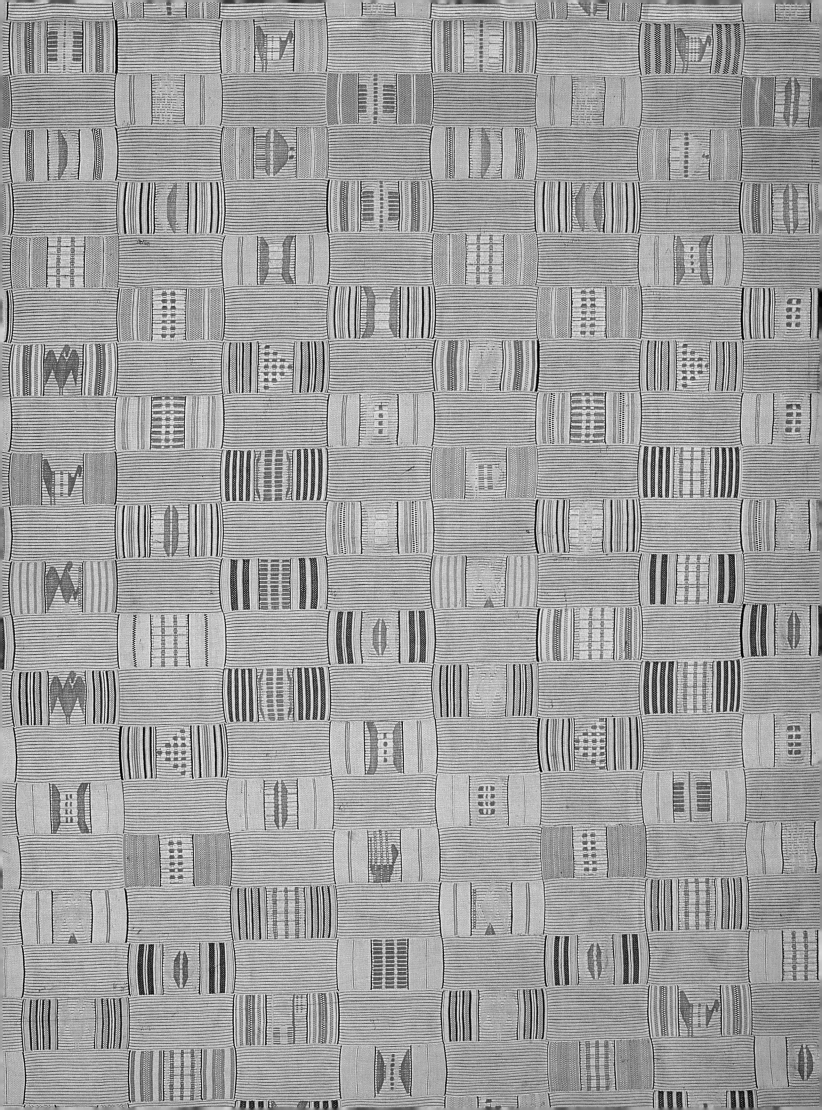

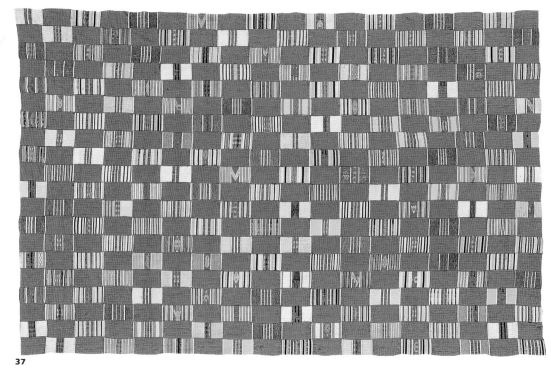

37

38

39

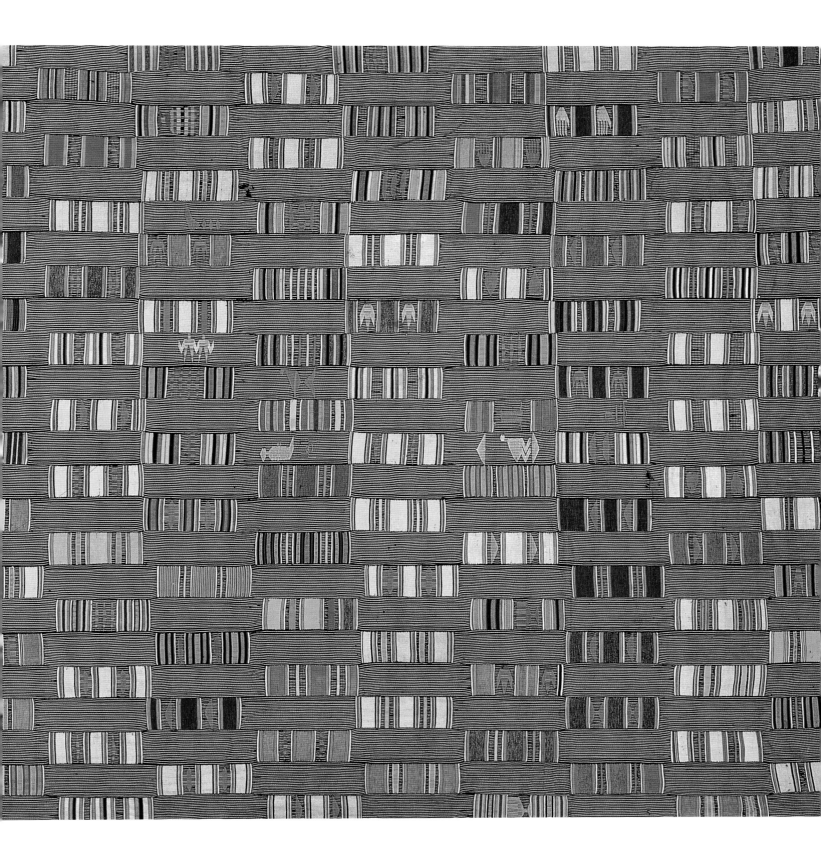

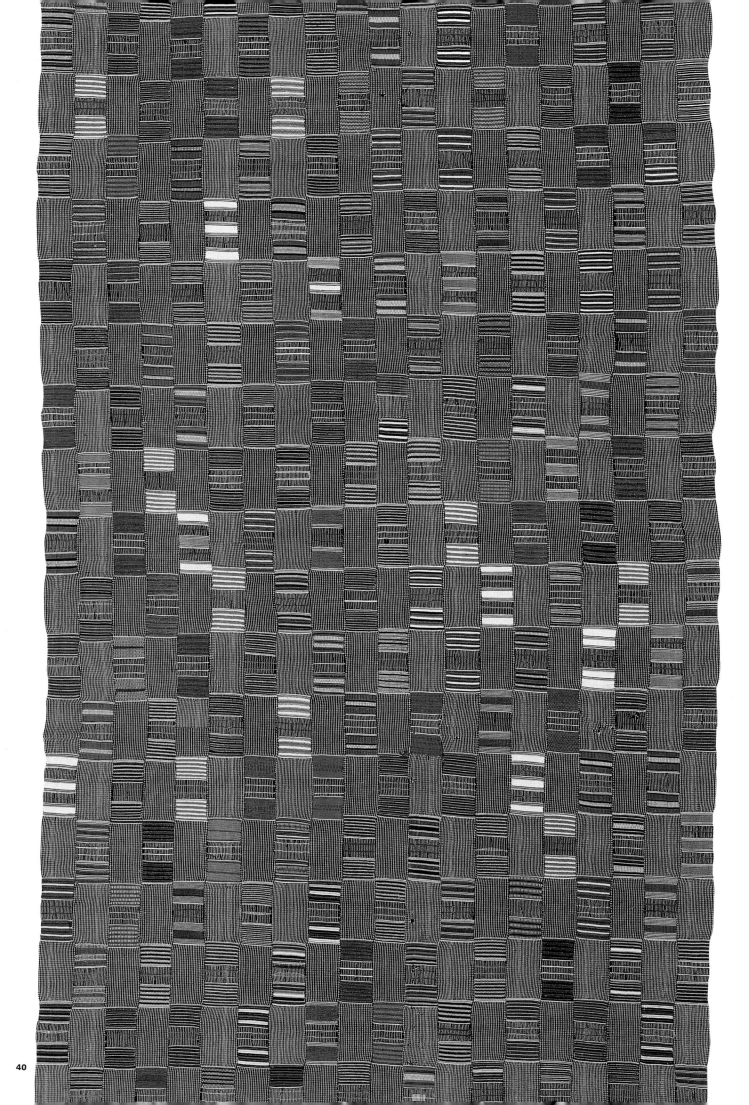

41

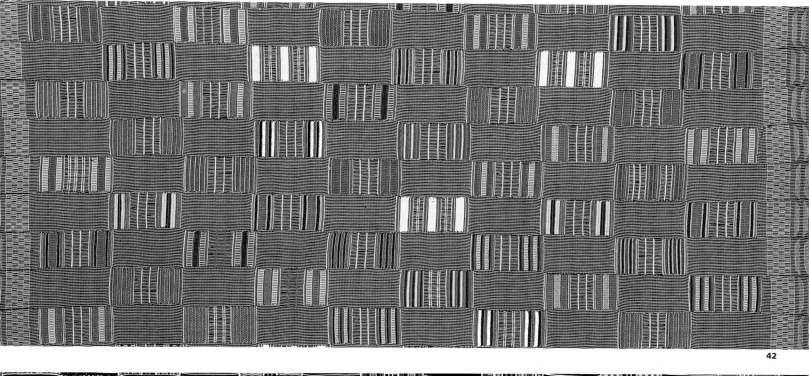

42

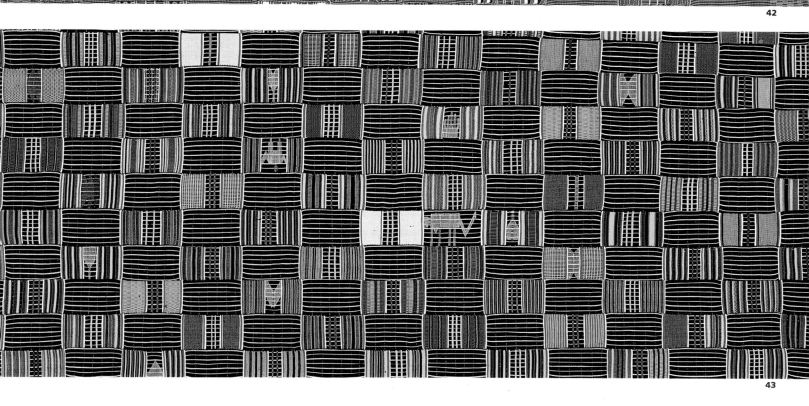

43

44–47

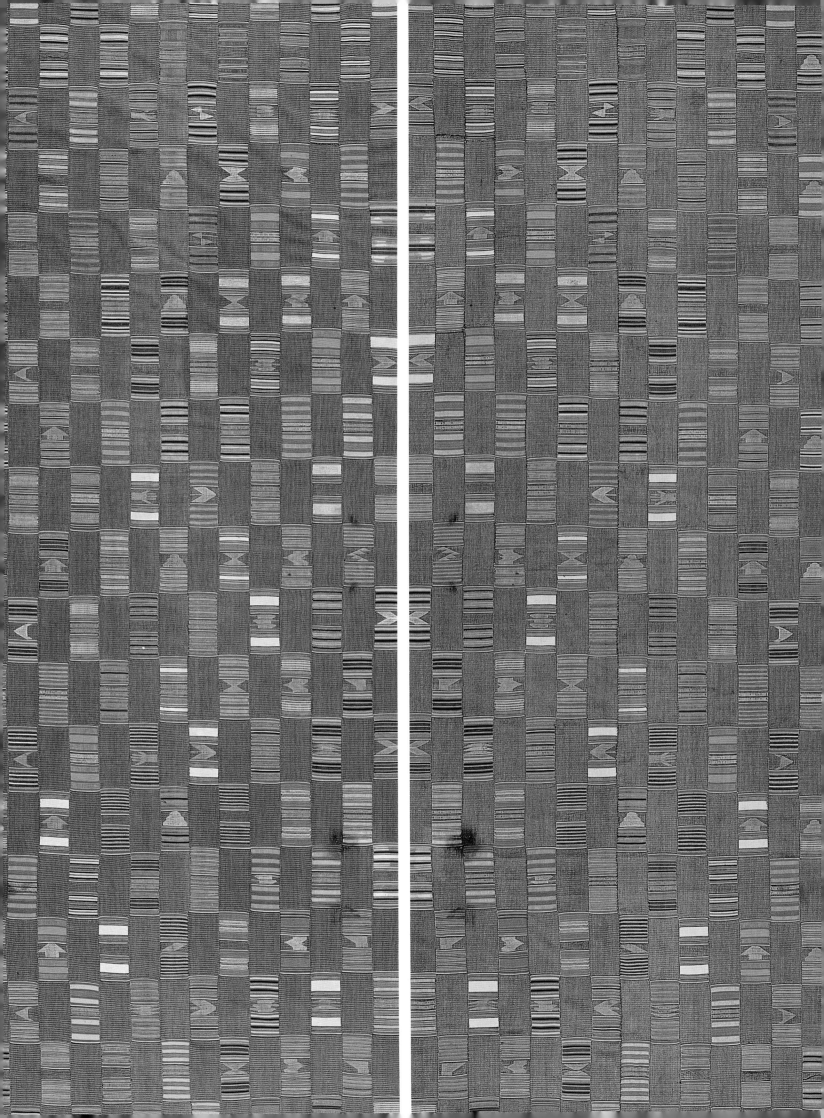

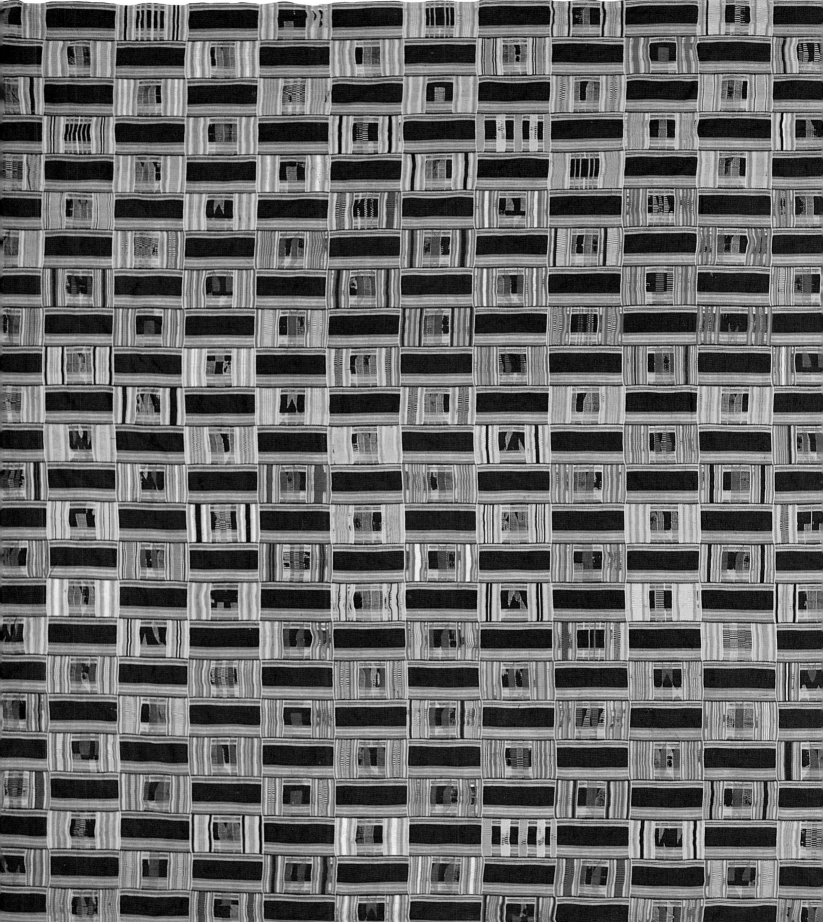

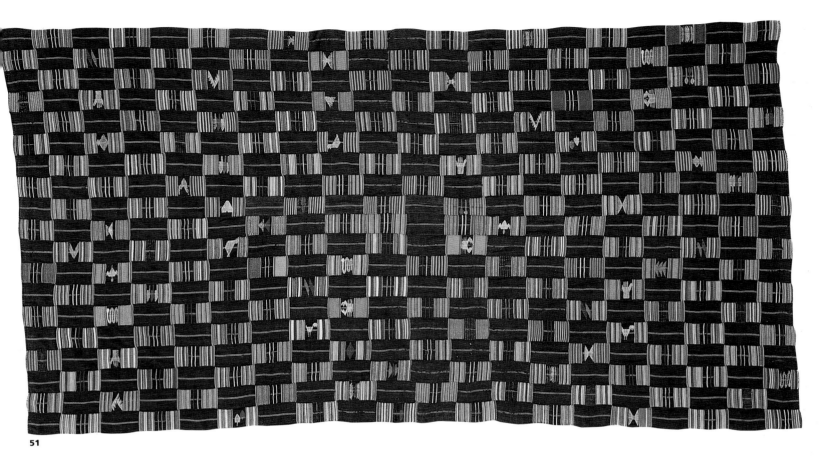

51

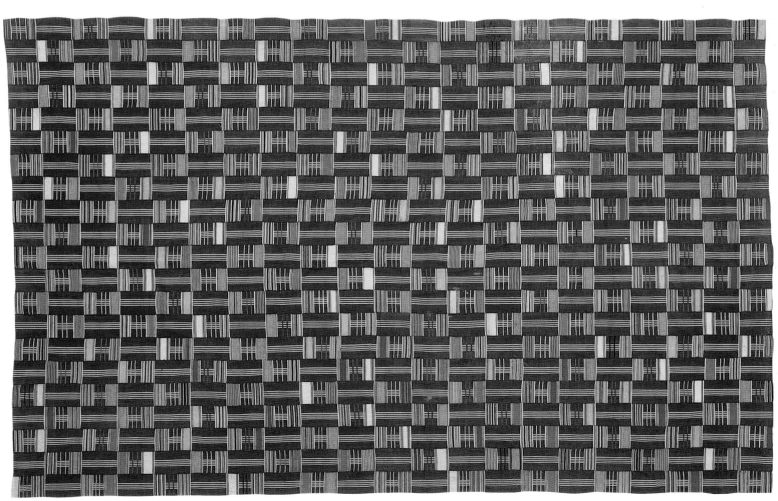

52

53

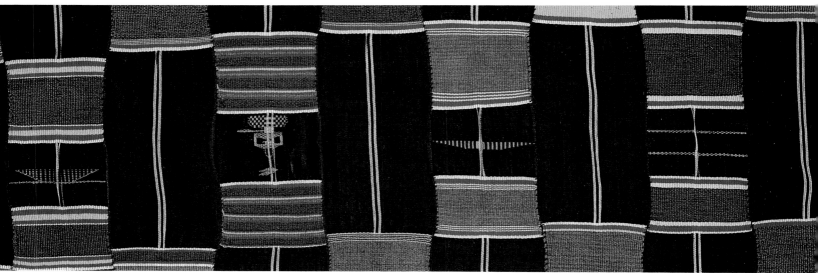

54

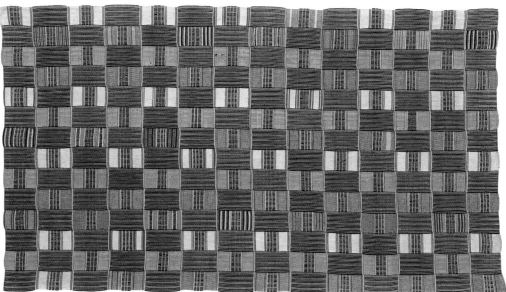

55

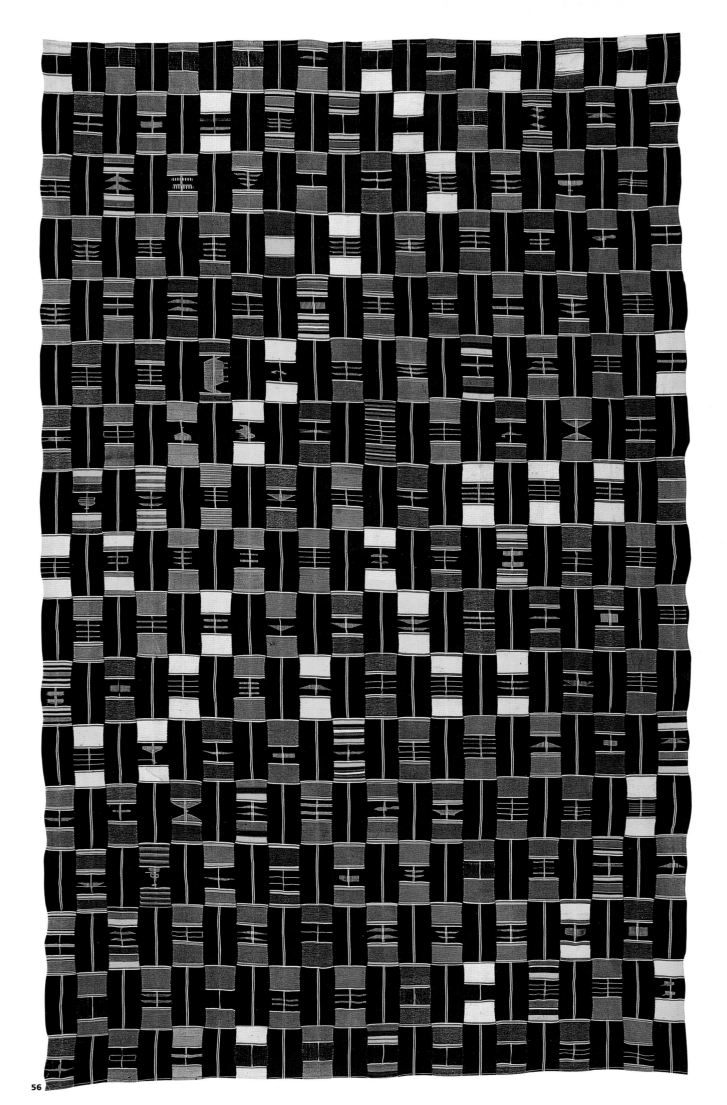

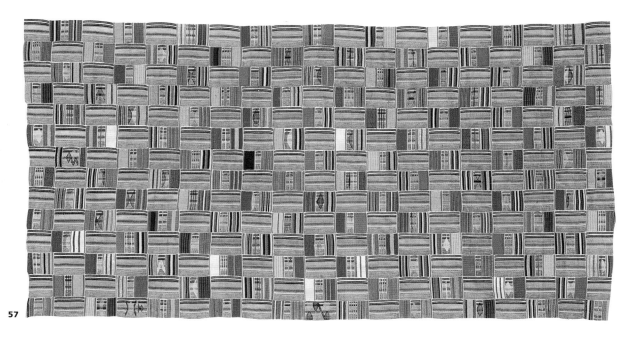

57

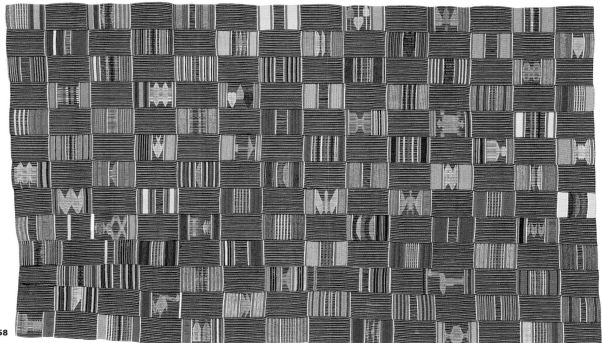

58

59

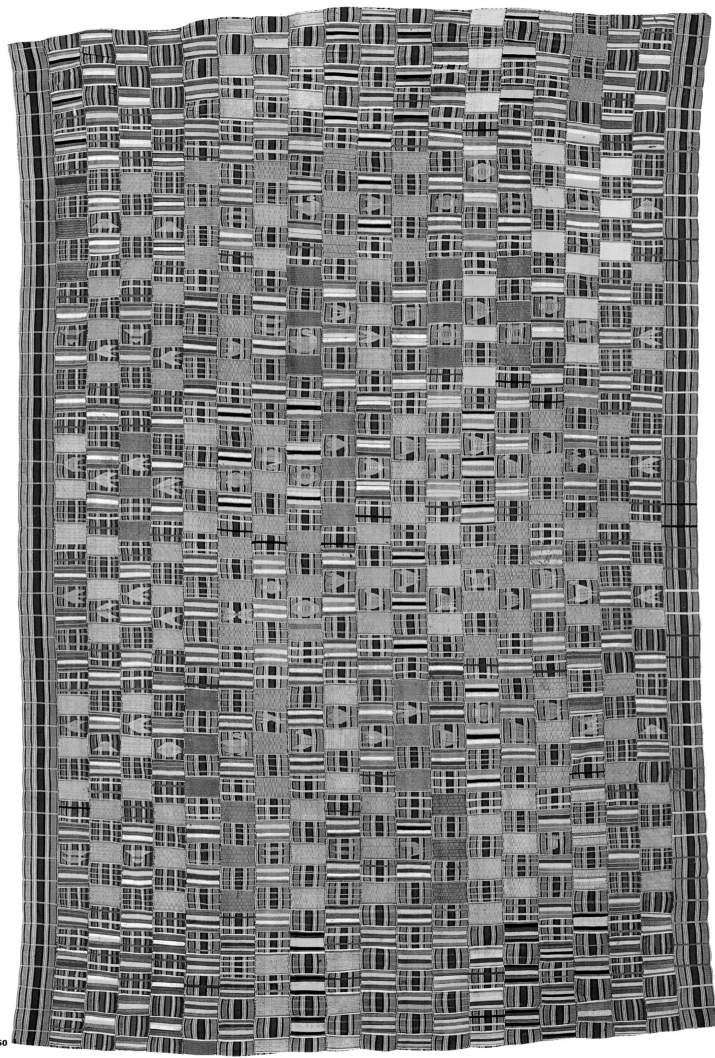

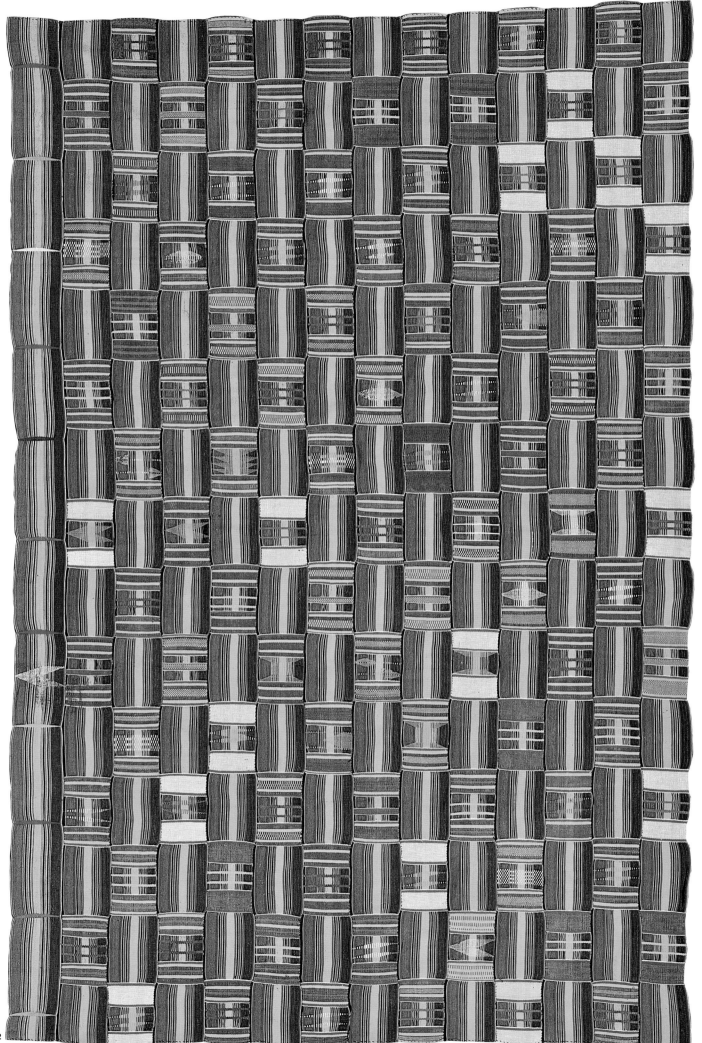

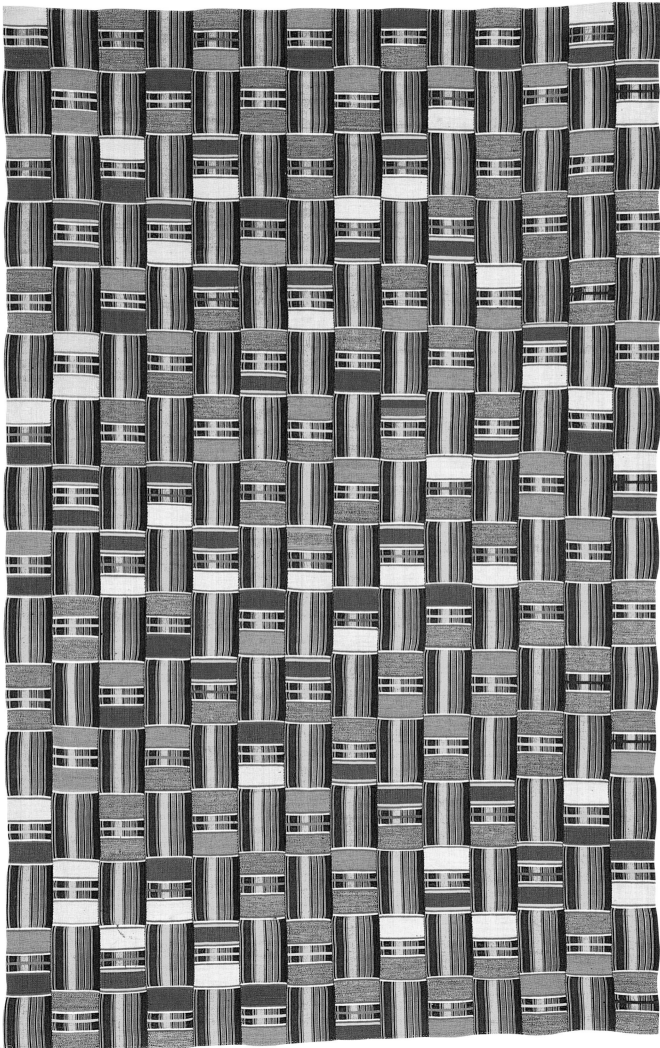

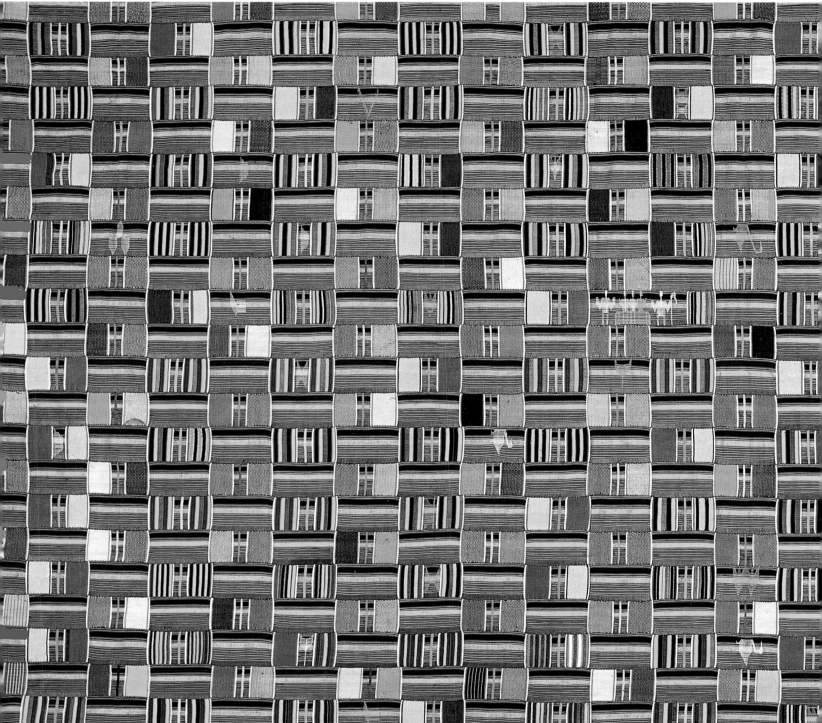

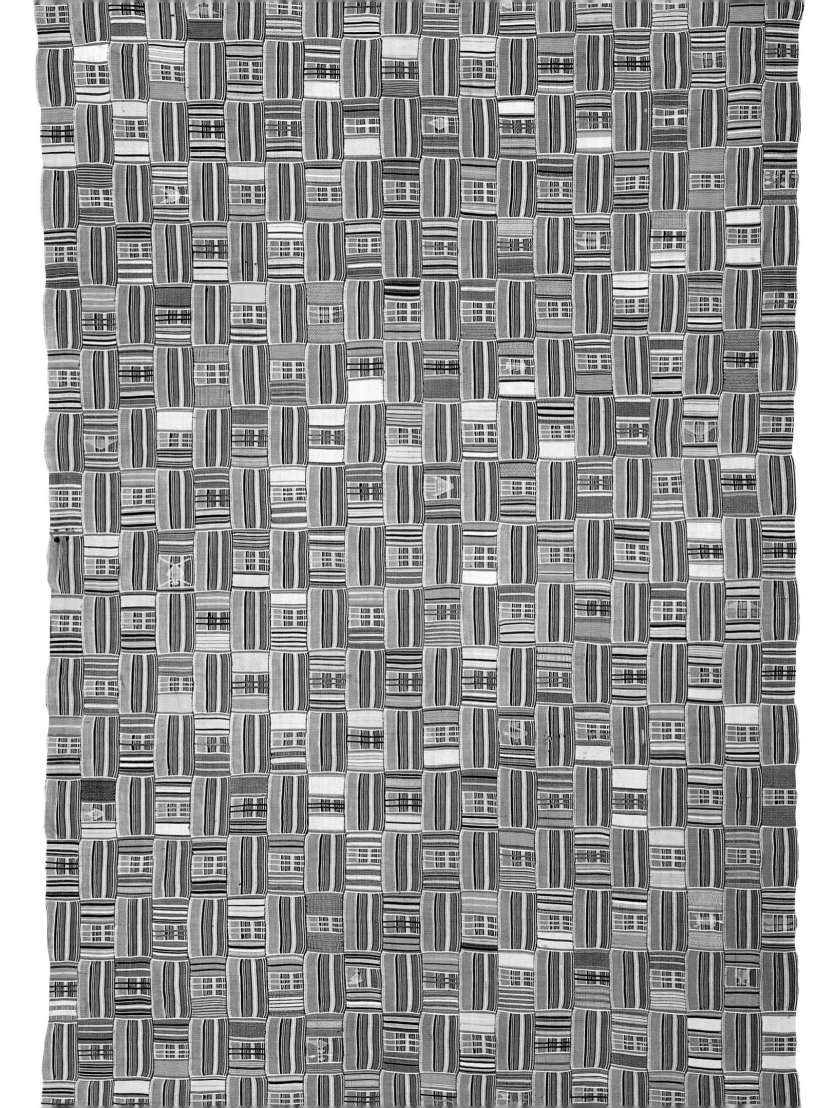

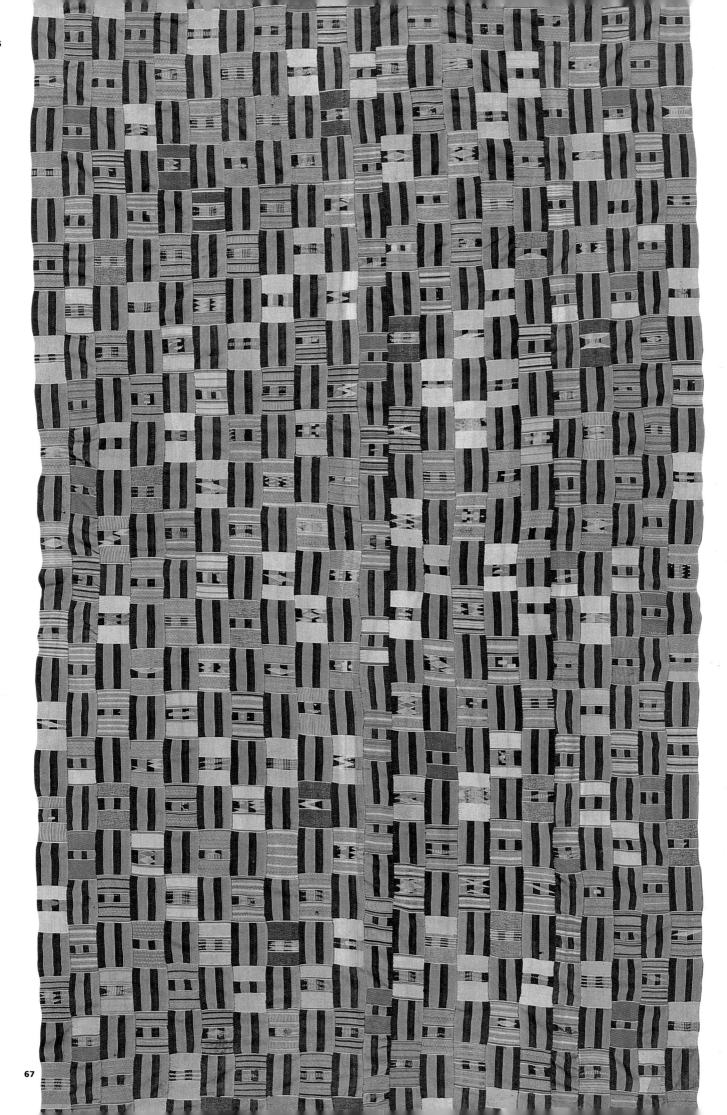

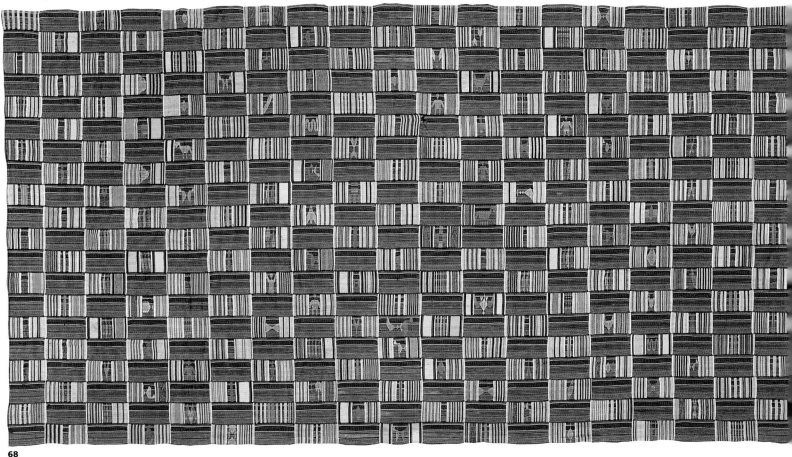

68

69

70 ▷

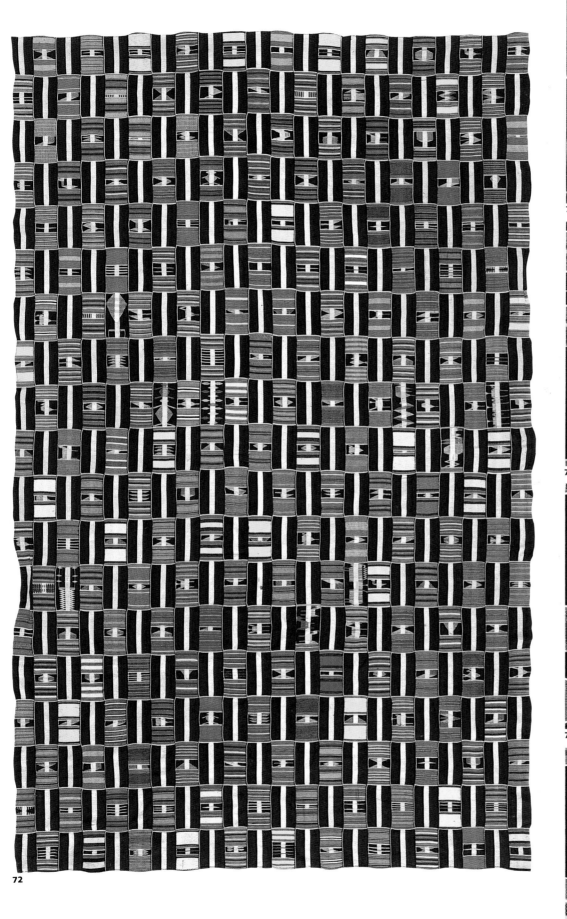

72

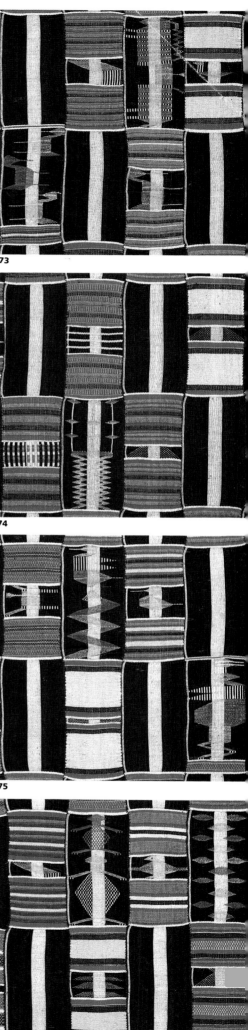

73

74

75

76

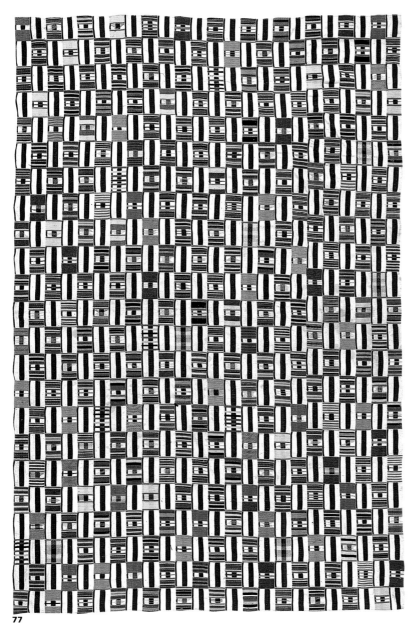

77

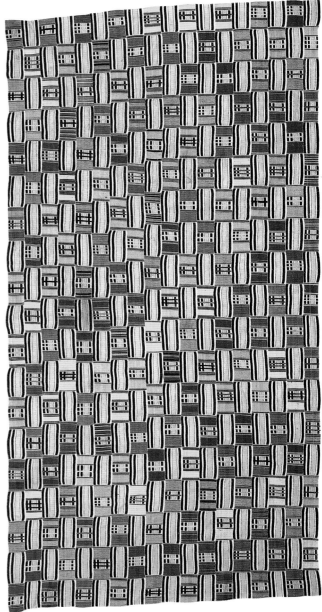

78

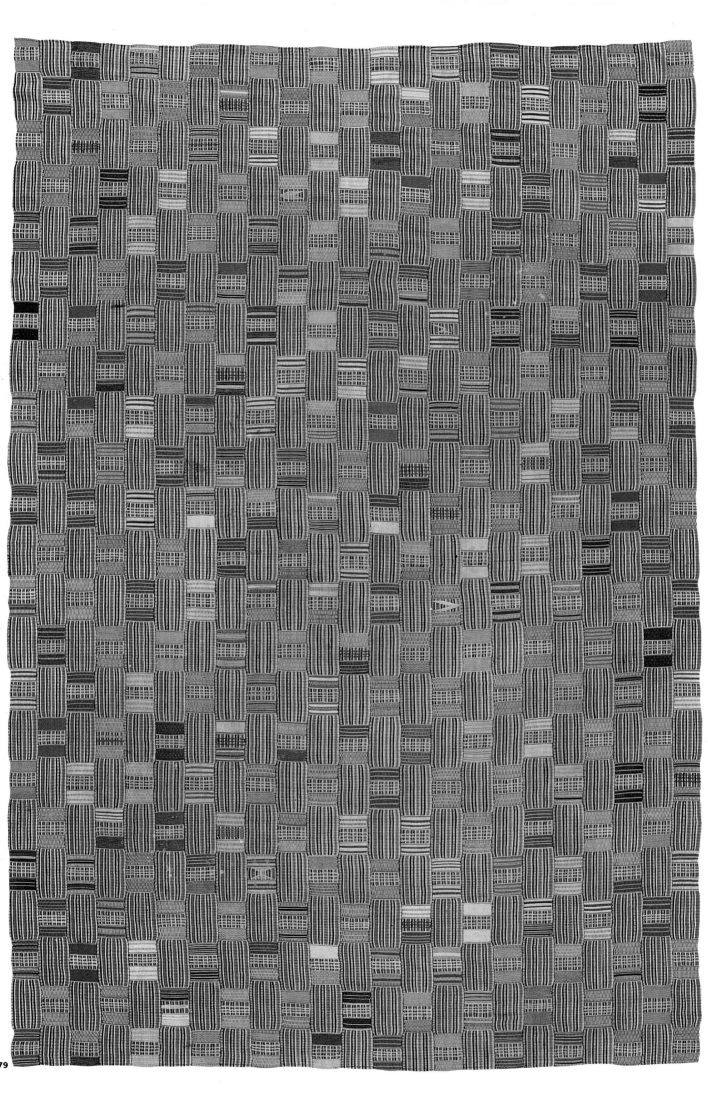

4

The Ewe cloth

ACROSS TO THE EAST AND THE SOUTH-EAST OF GHANA and on into the lands of Togo, the Ewe people are to be found. Unlike the Ashanti, who owe their demographic origins to the central forest region of Ghana and much of their cultural identity to the northerly influences of the Savannah, the Ewe came from afar and, on settling, borrowed much from the dominant group in their newly adopted region. Throughout their relatively recent history of occupation of the Volta river area, the overlords have always been the Ashanti, and it has, therefore, been the constant interplay of influences between the Ashanti craftsmen and the Ewe strip-weavers that has driven the development of both weaving cultures.

The Ewe of the Volta region of Ghana consider their lands of origin as lying somewhere within the present-day borders of Nigeria, Benin and Togo; Ewe traditions claim that in the distant past there was a diaspora from the Niger basin area centred on the towns of Oyo or Ketu, where the Yoruba now predominate. The Ewe are thought to have migrated westwards from the early sixteenth century onwards, inspired perhaps by the competitive territorial expansion of the Yoruba. The Volta river proved to be the strategic divide between the path of the shifting Ewe and the newly emergent Ashanti empire. Once within the Volta basin, the Ewe group seems to have divided into three main bodies; the largest, the Anlo, settled at the mouth of the Volta, and the two remaining groups established themselves further north, around Hohoe and Kpandu. By the seventeenth century the Ewe had largely occupied the lands of their present domain, a total area that runs 50 miles (80 kilometres) eastwards from the Volta along the coast and 100 miles (160 kilometres) north, forming the south-eastern corner of Ghana, which abuts on Togo. This natural divide of the Volta, which once formed the border between the German colony of Togoland, established in 1884, and the British-controlled Gold Coast, established in 1874, as well as marking the longer-standing Ewe and Akan division, was made meaningless by the territorial carve-up that followed the First World War. France and Britain shared the German colonial lands as spoils, and in 1919 what had been German Togoland was divided along a north–south axis. The Ewe were, in consequence, divided, the western group becoming part of the Gold Coast.

The Ewe have undoubtedly been strip-weavers since well before their sixteenth- and seventeenth-century migrations, and must have carried their own style of highly portable heddles, comb and tools to their new point of settlement. Once they were established in the areas where they reside today, their main source of trading, cultural and political influence would have been Kumasi and 'the eye-opening lands' of the Ashanti and other Akan groups. Towards the west, the land that became the Gold Coast offered trade; to the east, what had been the Slave Coast held no attraction. Even though the prohibitive costs imposed by the late nineteenth-century customs policy of the British forced the Ewe to ally with the Germans, rather than trade with the more successful Ashanti, their ever-developing culture had already been deeply infiltrated by Akan mores and practices.

Despite their numbers and their geographical spread, the Ewe have never united to form an autocratic kingdom. The many sub-tribes have no central focus and function as separate patrilineages. Contact with the Ashanti and associated Akan cultures has, however, provided the overlay of a chieftain-dominated social structure. The few early European routes to the interior were established by those seeking the gold of the forest lands or pathways to Timbuktu, and so the Ewe, like many major tribal groups of West Africa, were eclipsed by the attention lavished on the Ashanti and the lands of the Niger river bend. The history of the Ewe and of their weaving in particular is, therefore, not surprisingly, almost non-existent. For the weaving historians this is particularly frustrating; for devotees of colour and pattern it is of no consequence. As the colour plates in this book reveal, whatever their past history, the Ewe strip-weavers of the nineteenth and early to mid-twentieth century were able to express their creative and technical skills in cloth with imagination, artistry and ingenuity that are without equal.

From the limited reports that do exist it is possible to discern that the Ewe have been weavers of great quantities of cloth, of varying qualities, for a marketplace well beyond their borders for many centuries. Not constrained by the limitations of a court-dominated social order or by the restricted supply of cotton yarns, as their Ashanti counterparts were, the entrepreneurial Ewe weavers have become the major suppliers of cloth to West Africa, satisfying their private commission clients and bulk-buyers of cloth alike. At the time of the American Civil War, as the cotton production of the southern states was disrupted, the Ewe were one of the cultures approached by Europeans hoping to trade in the supply of cotton. They met with no success; the Ewe were too busy weaving with all their own supplies and with the yarns obtained from the Savannah lands to the north! The European missionaries of the mid-nineteenth century tell of many weavers being active in the Ewe lands; the air was disturbed by the noise of their looms, and the state of activity was compared with that of a Victorian workshop or mill.

Weavers of great creative and design flexibility, supplying a diverse client base across southern West Africa, the Ewe have proved to be great copyists. This quality has ensured that the Ewe have always been quick to respond to the demands of the market, which of late has called for 'Ashanti'-style strip-weaves. One of the driving forces behind this specific trend is associated with the corporate gift fad of newly independent Ghana. In the 1960s and '70s there was a fashion for Ghanaian businesses to dispense as gifts many hundreds of strip-weaves, woven in the style of the imperial and dominant tribe of the land, the Ashanti. The production of such a quantity of cloth would have been a physical impossibility for the Ashanti alone, as well as being culturally unacceptable to the proud elders and senior Ashanti weavers, who were determined to maintain traditional standards. The Ewe proved to be capable and efficient suppliers of more than adequate copies to meet the order. And so the Ewe have tended to become well known for their imitation of Ashanti strip-weave colours and patterns; their own highly original, excellent quality cloths have been ignored until very recently.

From a study of the range of the cloths it is immediately obvious that the Ewe are not mere replicators, and that they enjoy as proud a weaving tradition as any other West African strip-weaving group of note. The Ashanti would bristle at such boastful claims by the Ewe; one Ewe weaver retorted that he would not sell a fine cloth, even to the Asantehene, so zealously did he wish Ewe designs to be protected, and it is common lore that the Ewe see themselves as the original inventors of the strip-weave phenomenon in the region and that they claim to have taught the Ashanti all they know.

Unlike their Ashanti weaving compatriots, the Ewe know no bounds in their desire to satisfy the market forces of fashion and price, and so their production of strip-weaves is very varied indeed. Rather than restricting himself, like the Ashanti weaver, to the few hundred 'traditional' ground-weave pattern colours of the past – a range that has now been reduced by a lack of quality demand to only a few score in common use today – the Ewe weaver has allowed his imagination free rein, meeting the demands of the market with an innovatory flourish. There are, therefore, many hundreds of different Ewe ground-weave patterns, which appear and disappear with great rapidity. Many of the colour combinations do, necessarily, mimic the well-known and popular Ashanti patterns, and are repeated on demand. The overall lack of continuity in design and colour is, however, vital and exciting, and preferable to the creative stagnation that has befallen their Ashanti weaving neighbours.

In contrast to the Ashanti production of the late twentieth century, the Ewe continue to weave the majority of their cloths with cotton yarn. One of the reasons for the wide-ranging scope of the Ewe ground-weave patterns is the ready availability of dyed yarn in many colours. It is certain that the early Ewe production, like that of the Ashanti, was predominantly blue and white cloth made of cotton of local and Savannah origin, which was then enlivened by the much sought-after bright colours, such as red and yellow, unravelled from the trade cloth from Europe and India. Rather than follow the path to silken luxury of the wealthy Ashanti, the Ewe have developed their use of fine, bright-coloured cottons with verve. The fact that, until recently, they obtained quantities of such cotton yarns from the northern market towns suggests an important cross-cultural relationship between the Ewe and the weavers of the Savannah.

Unfortunately, both the Ashanti and the Ewe groups share a common problem today: the supply of poor quality yarns. The silk, and silk and synthetic blends of yarn that arrive from China and Japan are expensive. More importantly, very little hand-spun cotton is now produced in the

Volta region or brought in from the once cotton-rich areas of the Upper Volta (Burkina Faso) and northern Ghana itself. The cotton stuffs supplied to the Ewe weavers today are from the mills of Ghana, the Ivory Coast, England or India; all is machine-spun and coloured with synthetic dyes. The quality of yarn produced by modern methods can never hope to replicate the feel or the tones of the cloths of the pre-industrial past. The increased range of colours available is a spur for the imagination, however, and when the yarn is well spun and colour-fast, the results are more than adequate. It is the coarse yarn and the fugitive dyestuffs of cheap modern production that have ruined the quality of much of the commercial weaving of the Ewe.

The Ewe, like the Ashanti, produce a variety of qualities of cloth. Essentially, these can be divided into two categories. Firstly, there are the commercial cotton cloths and yardage that is predominantly plain, in simple combinations of blue, red and white, of wine red, blue and white, or dark green, blue and white. This cotton material is manufactured in very great quantities for sale to local consumers and, more importantly, to the Muslim cloth traders of the region, who peddle such wares across the whole of southern West Africa. Some of the better qualities of this cloth might be compared to the N'tama of the Ashanti, and inlay patterning on these weaves is either absent altogether, or rarely exceeds the complexity of the single-weave Ashanti Topreko or Faprenu weaves, with their very widely scattered small inlay motifs. This cloth is the everyday attire of the Ewe of means, and has considerable value as 'traditional' cloth used to shroud funeral litters and to create a hanging textile enclave for the corpse within a dwelling or compound.

The second, and superior grade of cloth is woven on a commission basis only, and is therefore reserved for the use of wealthier members of the Ewe and adjacent communities enamoured of such richly patterned and coloured cloth. Lamb calls this cloth 'Adanudo', from the Ewe 'Adanu', meaning skilled or wise, and 'Do' meaning cloth. It is predominantly made of high-grade cotton, although examples of silk and rayon are known. This production may be compared with the Ashanti Nsaduaso, and like the Ashanti weaves, the Adanudo background weave is patterned with blocks of colour that contain single and double inlay motifs in the *babadua* style. Although the

Ashanti cloths often contain some figurative or figuratively derived motifs that have become geometrically abstracted, the Ewe Adanudo cloths are, by contrast, very often awash with clearly discernable representational characters.

In Ewe, as opposed to Ashanti society there is no royal or superior prerogative for the use and display of so specialized a quality of cloth, but, like the Ashanti, the Ewe display their cloth at social gatherings such as weddings, funerals and 'enthronements' of chiefs. Anyone may order an Adanudo cloth to be woven, and it is not surprising that most of the clients are chiefs and elders. A client will, therefore, commission a cloth at a price that he can afford and to a quality and range of patterns for which the weaver is well known. Payment is usually in two stages, one half paid at the commission stage and the balance on delivery. Women may commission two smaller cloths, to be worn as a skirt and a wrap, although this fashion seems to be largely moribund.

For the Ashanti weavers, the hinterland of Bonwire is their home, but by contrast the Ewe weavers are found throughout their eastern Ghana and Togo borderlands, and it is common, when driving along the track that shadows the territorial divide, to find groups, as well as lone weavers, at work in many villages along the 40-mile (64-kilometre) journey. Lamb has distinguished three groups of Ewe weavers by the style of their production: to the north, the Central-Ewe, around Hohoe and Kpandu; in the centre around Kpetoe (pronounced 'Petwai'), the Ewe-Adangbe, and to the south the Ewe-Anlo. It is the work of the Ewe-Adangbe and, to a much lesser extent, the Ewe-Anlo, that forms the most original and colourful content of this book. Of these two groups, there is no doubt that the southern coastal Ewe of the Volta river estuary lands, loosely defined as the Anlo, are the most prolific manufacturers of all.

The term Anlo encompasses many Ewe sub-groups, including the Afife, Avenor, Dzodze, Fenyi, Klikor, Sommé and Weta. The Anlo themselves inhabit the lands around Keta Lagoon, and Lamb estimated in 1975 that there were as many as four thousand weavers within this group alone: 'but there are even more weavers among the other groups listed above who produce a cloth that cannot in any meaningful way be distinguished from that of Anlo.' The historical preeminence of this latter group is substantiated by the fact that the town of Keta was, from at least the eighteenth century, the centre of supply for Anlo trade weaves often known as 'Keta cloth'. Keta has been in sharp decline as a weaving market town for over thirty years, however, owing to changes in the routing of the Volta river which have isolated the coastal strip. The new centre of Ewe-Anlo cloth trade is located at the town of Agbozume, conveniently located on the mainland near the Togo border and astride the main coast road.

Agbozume is the central town of the Sommé people, one of the Ewe-Anlo groups, and a visit to this lively and happy market is a rewarding experience. Hundreds of weavers' wives congregate in a babbling mass of colourful activity, bargaining to sell the products of their husbands' work, which is stacked in rolls of stripes at their feet. These tightly wrapped lengths of cloth are all strip-woven and hand-sewn as ready-to-wear men's and women's robes, and such is the quantity available that the market square is alive with the smattering of Arabic of the Hausa traders and their Yoruba counterparts from the north and east respectively. The Ewe-Anlo cloths are then traded far and wide across West Africa. From the sheer quantity of cloth available and the style of its manufacture, it is immediately obvious that the Ewe-Anlo production supplies a large market for 'everyday' and 'traditional' cloth. That is not to say that the purchase of this type of strip-weave is anything less than a major investment for most buyers in West Africa, yet a comparison of the Ewe-Anlo with the work of the Ashanti and, as will be seen, the work of the Ewe-Adangbe, is that between the everyday production of simply woven cloth that is a luxury for the poorer people, and the small-scale production of commissioned work that results in a highly decorated luxury consumable for the very privileged and the wealthy.

Most of the production from the Ewe-Anlo weavers' looms is of rather sombre colour combinations of green, burgundy, blue, red and white stripes. The pattern of the cloth is derived from the warp arrangement alone, and many of these stripes are exceedingly narrow, creating a dark and dense atmosphere to the composition. Such is the large-scale, lower-income demand for this 'traditional' style of simple striped cloth that the Ewe-Anlo weavers are in the unusual position of maintaining the creative qualities of their strip-weaving ancestors with a healthy vigour. The commissioned cotton cloth of the Adanudo variety is influenced by the ever-changing demands of fashion. It is either of the striped variety, enlivened by a scattered arrangement of abstract double-weft inlays in rayon, which may appear as stars, diamonds and broken bands of bright colour, or of an 'older style', made of plain cotton, silk or rayon and patterned with naturalistic animals and objects which run along the warp. Such cloth often shimmers with the unusual and striking colours of the figures – vivid blue, yellow or lime green, speckled with red, black, white, green and blue – which are created in a minutely detailed double weft technique. In this way cats, guns, lizards, swords, cows, forks, fish, humans, birds, lizards and chiefs' stools run across the cloth with dramatic effect. Lamb noted that one cloth contained seventy-four different pictorial inlays.

Such work is now rarely seen, and aside from the market cloth of simple warp stripes, the quality production has been corrupted of late by the desire to copy certain characteristics of the popular Ashanti cloths, with indifferent results. Acid-bright colours clash with each other in the warp, while the weft inlays are inelegantly executed and show little variety. Pictorial representations of animals are absent, and the random, varied compositions have been replaced by cloths decorated with machine-like repetitiveness. The irony of this circumstance is poignant, for as the attention of the discerning consumer wanders from the creatively bankrupt Ashanti production of today, so the Ewe-Anlo Adanudo weavers are in no position to offer their traditionally spirited and original compositions, having been corrupted in the recent past by their mimicry of the Akan work for necessary commercial gain.

Just before the road that follows the Ghana and Togolese border turns westwards, and within an area of mixed forest and savannah, one passes through the large village of Agotime Kpetoe. As a collection of buildings that cluster about the road, there is little to distinguish Kpetoe from many other West African villages. On alighting from a car on a fine day, however, one is aware of a rustling murmur in the air that is disjointed yet rhythmical. It is the sound of the combs, the shuttles and weaving swords at work on scores of drag looms throughout the village. Tucked away on the far eastern side of Ghana and straddling the border, Agotime Kpetoe is the little-known source of the finest Adanudo cloth of the Ewe; their strip-woven cloth forms the visual centrepiece of this book and represents a particular era of Ewe creativity that fused diverse influences with brilliant results.

'Ago' is Ewe for the fan palm, 'ti' is tree and 'me' is translated as inside or in. At the place of the fan palm, then, reside the Ewe and their more recently arrived weaving companions, the Ga-speaking Adangbe. By a somewhat indirect route, which included dwelling sites on the coast of the Gold Coast, the Adangbe migrated to the Volta region from Central Togo from about the eighteenth century. The more recent Adangbe migrants in the vicinity of Agotime Kpetoe and Agotime Akpokofe have arrived within the last one hundred years. The 'original' Adangbe of central Togo are known strip-weavers, and so there has been a positive fusion of two creative cultures. From the xenophobic point of view of an Ewe story-teller, it seems that as a result of the intermingling processes, such as intermarriage, the Ewe and the Adangbe may now, in the late twentieth century, be considered one larger Ewe group. Indeed, Ewe is the established language of the area today. Naturally, however, the Adangbe claim to be the oldest established weavers of the region and insist that they were the ones who instructed both the Ashanti and the Ewe in the craft.

Whatever their roots, the weavers of these villages are known for the high quality of their output, which is primarily very colourful Adanudo cloth that is woven to commission; there is no weaving market, as at Agbozume, or quantity production of ready-to-wear cloth. The region has not been immune, however, to the change in market forces that has beset their Ewe companions to the south and the Ashanti within the forest to the west. A lack of quality commissions and the demand for Ashanti imitations has driven many weavers to settle closer to the market at Accra, and there is pressure for the production at Kpetoe to focus much energy on producing tourist wares such as crudely inlaid sashes. Very few Adanudo cloths of the colour range, quality and style of those depicted here are made today. Such, however, has been the pace of development in style of the Ewe and Adangbe weavers over the past two hundred years that there is no reason why such skills cannot be rekindled, given a resurrection in 'quality' demand, most likely driven by an export and gallery-associated interest.

The Adanudo cloths illustrated here, woven between 150 and 20 years ago, display the superior imagination of the Ewe-Adangbe group in manipulating colour within a field of strip-woven bands. It seems, however, that like the Ashanti, the Ewe-Adangbe have evolved their colourful palette, decorated with precise weft inlays, from simple compositions of blocks in few colours. Today the Ewe-Adangbe weavers seem to have peaked in a frenzy of design and colour expression, but in Kpetoe it is still possible to view some examples of the 'older' and 'simpler' style. These are densely woven cotton blankets which may be about 150 years old or more. The cotton is of the imported and unravelled European variety, and the cloth is heavy, more akin to a blanket in weight. The compositions are simple, striking and memorable: a repeating chequerboard of small and plain squares, undecorated with weft inlays and employing no more than two or three combinations of yellow, white, red and green. The wefts are beaten down hard so that the warps are hidden and only the weft colour is visible. This kind of composition and technique has a distinct 'northern' feel, reminiscent of the work of the weavers of the Niger river bend.

How and when the next stage of pattern evolution occurred is open to conjecture. What is clear is that the strips of weft-patterned 'checks' were broken up into narrow bands, so that any warp stripes could be seen as the background design structure to the cloth within the intervals between the bands. Within these rectangles weft inlay patterns of both an abstract and a representational character were woven. This style of decoration is similar to that of the Ashanti, and the cloths may therefore be described as having *babadua* weft bands of colour, between which are inserted Topreko single-weave motifs, where the background pattern can still be discerned, or Faprenu double-weave patterns, which obscure the warp stripes. It is by the use of cotton rather than silk, in the seemingly haphazard array of figurative and geometric inlay forms, by the colour associations and the arrangement of the weft bands and blocks that the Ewe-Adangbe show their compositional ingenuity.

In contrast to the Ashanti cloths of any description, the colour blocks and bands of the Ewe-Adangbe very rarely repeat each other across the field. Although they follow the *susudua* style of regular matching of weft inlay blocks with adjacent undecorated warp areas, the colours of the inlays are varied so that the cloth appears to be constantly 'on the move', and the eye is not hindered by the matching repetitiveness of the composition. Again, the Ewe-Adangbe reveal their preference for dynamic energy and 'movement' in a cloth by often allowing the arrangement of the blocks to slip, creating a diagonal of weft blocks across the cloth or, when the design is taken to the extreme, an abstract composition of colour blocks. In this way the regularity of the *susudua*, a pattern technique that so often conveys tension, is broken up, and the cloth shimmers with colour in movement.

Unlike the old Ewe-Anlo Adanudo cloths, in which the composition is created by lively and detailed representations of animals, birds, humans and inanimate forms, set against a background of plain stripes, the Ewe-Adangbe pictorial weft inlays are only one part of the overall energy of the cloth. At times the cloths are so packed with animal representations that the strips run like some circus cavalcade; on other cloths there are only a few motifs placed seemingly without thought, yet adding to the overall impact of the textile. The quantity and type of motifs on a cloth seems to be devised by the weaver alone, and unlike the Ashanti, there are no exclusive preserves of weaving style. The Ewe-Adangbe weaver has always been left to decorate a cloth to please himself and the desires of the client; there are no conventions to be followed, save the dictates of fashion or the collective symbology and style of the group of weavers to which he belongs. Without a doubt, the clients for such Adanudo cloths would tend to be of chiefly extraction, elders or wealthy men – or combinations of all three – and so the choice of motifs by the weaver has to match the status of such senior figures. The paraphernalia of rank are often in evidence; chiefs' stools are common, as are swords, umbrellas and men holding staffs of office.

We will never know precisely how the Ewe-Adangbe developed so rich and colourful a decorative style of strip-weaving within less than two hundred years. As weavers of fine cotton cloths unrestricted by the regulations and codes of conduct of the Kumasi-centred Ashanti court, the Ewe, and later the Ewe-Adangbe, have been in a privileged position. Looking westwards towards the splendour of the Ashanti, the Ewe desired to mimic the colour of their court, and without the means to import silks, developed a sophisticated expression with cotton. Such influences may well have been reinforced or developed by contact with the Adangbe and their weaving and compositional skills. Lamb, by contrast, sees the representational inlays of the Ewe as being inspired by the work of the Djerma of Burkina Faso, Niger and northern Dahomey, who sometimes pattern their cloth with motifs that are strikingly similar to those of the weavers of Kpetoe. From all these observations it is obvious that the Ewe have been open to many influences from all points of the compass. It has been their genius to synthesize these ingredients in order to produce such a majestic collection of cloth.

5

The looms and materials

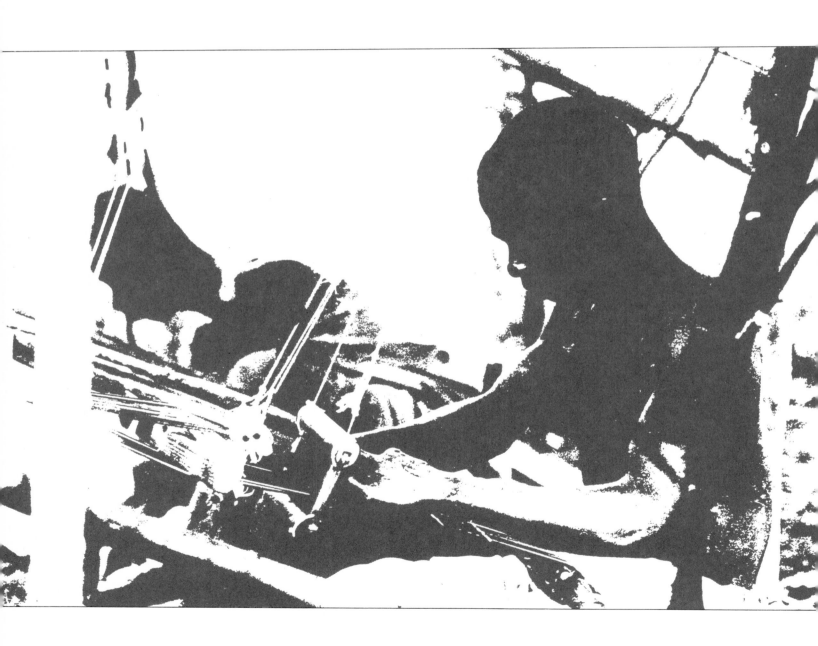

STRIP-WEAVING IS A TECHNIQUE ADOPTED BY MANY textile cultures of the world to facilitate the practice of a useful craft without restricting the mobility of the group. Narrow strip looms are small in size, easy and quick to dismantle and very simple to operate: ideal technical and structural considerations for the nomad. For weavers such as the Uzbek women of north Afghanistan and the Shahsavan of the north Iranian plains, it is at the time of the summer encampments that they can weave their bands of woollen cloth outside. Seated on the ground before a simple tripod loom, they produce warp-faced strips that may be sewn together as a cover or used as a lashing for the tents and pack animals.

When they are ready to move on or to return to the wintering grounds, the whole apparatus is dismantled and rolled up for carriage on the camels or donkeys. More sedentary tribes have made adaptations to the tripod strip loom; on the Pakistan northern borders of the Hindu Kush, for example, the narrow-loom operator sits with his legs dangling in a pit, in which he operates the heddles. The strip-weavers of West Africa have selectively developed, over many centuries, the structural and technical possibilities of this type of loom for strip textile production to match their economic, religious and climatic needs.

The lot of the West African strip-weaver is clear; he owns very little working capital, either in yarnstuffs or weaving implements; he may journey to gather commissions from village to village; when at work, he must be able to remove the finished cloth and warps very easily at the first signs of a tropical rainstorm, as well as at the end of the day. Secure storage of the work in hand is not only financially important, but also, as will become clear, for reasons of religion and superstition.

The external structure of most of the Ashanti and Ewe strip looms is, therefore, exceedingly unsophisticated and of low value, and the heddles and pulley apparatus, warps and cloth may be removed in an instant. The weaver sits at his work on his own portable wooden stool, which is of either a traditional Akan or a simple design, specially built to place the worker at the most comfortable level to operate the heddles. Ewe looms are built of coarse yet elegantly arranged timbers, lashed together with string and rope; the whole arrangement is secured by uprights set

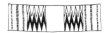

into the ground. When they are not in use, without the weaving paraphernalia, some of these frames look like free-standing wooden sculptures. Shaded protection from the sun is provided for the weaver by a palm frond-covered frame. The Ashanti seem to have refined their loom structure yet further, to create a semi-portable assembly, for many of the weavers work at looms that have been mounted on a flat wooden platform or decking. Weaving may therefore take place in any position that suits the worker, whether outdoors or, by manhandling the looms, indoors or on the shaded balcony of a house. The whole structure rests on the earth, concrete or tiled floor. The Ashanti looms tend to have an integral sunshade built onto the frame and, in contrast to the Ewe looms, are certainly more refined in finish. The wooden cross-members and uprights are sawn and planed with a precision that indicates the senior status of the Ashanti craftsmen amongst their West African counterparts.

A stroll through the villages of Bonwire or Kpetoe will leave the visitor in no doubt of the vitality of the Ashanti and Ewe weaving industry. In Bonwire the courtyards are lined with rows of weavers at their looms, and the houses and balconies echo to the sound of the shuttles and beaters clacking and rattling. The villages that surround Bonwire are home to other Ashanti weavers, working in smaller groups under their fronded shades. Kpetoe resonates with the energy of the weaving of the Ewe craftsmen, and all along the roads of the Volta delta area and inland, their weaving brothers are to be seen at work within their villages and hamlets.

Within all the weaving communities many side streets and alleyways are dotted by rows of poles up to 3 feet (1 metre) high; these wooden shafts or pegs, which are buried in the ground, are the warping poles. For an Ashanti man's cloth, which is invariably twenty-four strips wide and approximately 9 feet (2.7 metres) long, the line of poles for warping up is 95 feet (29 metres) long; for a smaller woman's cloth, a run of 66 feet (20 metres) is needed. The basic unit for warping up is a count of four threads, called 'oba' by the Ashanti, and the trained warper – a separate occupation to the weaver – will know by heart the count required for the arrangement of the colours to create a specified background warp pattern.

The yarn for the warping up process is wound onto large bobbins, which then slip over and rotate on the tines of the bobbin carrier; this is known as the 'menokomenam' by the Ashanti, which means 'I walk alone'. Holding this bobbin carrier before him, the warper strolls up and down the rows of poles, laying out the yarn and maintaining extreme vigilance in his placement of the threads, especially at the ends of the rows. At one end of the rows of poles is a pair of uprights, and it is onto these that the warps are crossed by hand and securely tied once the process is complete, so that the correct sequence of colours is maintained when the warps are removed and readied for threading through the heddles.

Ashanti and Ewe looms have two sets of heddles, which hang from pulleys on the wooden frame before the weaver. The first set of heddles is known as 'asatia' by the Ashanti and carries the background 'tabby' weave, alternate threads being passed through the leashes of each of the heddles in turn. This is known as a one-to-one thread-up. Fine cloth may contain some four to five hundred warp threads per strip, while the coarser weaves may have between two and three hundred. By crossing the leashes over when making up a heddle, the weaver forms a cross; this is the 'eye', which then supports the warp on its up or down cycle of movement. Threading up the heddles is a trying and fiddly business, and most weavers will squat on their haunches, using as many combinations of fingers, toes and thumbs as possible to assist with the correct arrangement of the apparent mess of warp threads before them.

The second set of heddles, the 'asanan' in Ashanti, are alternately threaded with bunches of six warp threads; these heddles are manipulated to create the inlay designs, carrying what is termed the six-to-six count pattern weave. It is by judicious and imaginative use of the *asanan* heddles that inlay patterns of a thickened weft in a count of six may be created, and it is with these patterns that the Ashanti and the Ewe give wonderful character to their cloths. Further inlay details may be inserted by creating an extra 'field' for the passage of coloured thread within a shuttle, or added by hand, by inserting a swordstick (the 'tabon' in Ashanti) through a combination of warps and turning it on its side. Such hand-picking is a frequent practice, and despite the labour-intensive nature of such detailing a good weaver can complete some 8 to 10 feet ($2\frac{1}{2}$ to 3 metres) of woven cloth per day. The Ewe are able to achieve their inlay patterns of floating wefts by hanging a fifth heddle from a top cross-beam of the loom. The twill weave of the royal Asasia cloth of the Ashanti is achieved by hanging a third set of heddles from the loom, and their manipulation, a complicated and dexterous act, slows the rate of weaving considerably.

Before sitting at his loom the weaver will complete the threading up process by passing the warp threads in groups of four between the bamboo or palm fibre teeth of the lightweight beater or reed, known as 'kyereye' by the Ashanti. Ewe and Ashanti reeds are very similar, having a heavier 'bowl' or lower section to the wooden frame to provide momentum for the swinging action of the operator. The combs are not only instrumental in tamping down the weft threads, but also ensure an even alignment to the warps and a straight edge.

The heddles are suspended on string and connected to the moveable top beam of the weaving frame by way of carved wooden pulleys, one to each pair of heddles. Each pair of heddles is tied together with a cord that runs up and down over the pulleys during the weaving process, and the heddles are manipulated by the toes of the worker; to the bowl of the heddle is attached a cord or string, which ends in a pedal made of a round of calabash or flip flop. These form the cups that are inserted between the big toe and the adjacent digit of the weaver, and the feet then operate in an alternate rhythm to open and close the sheds. Ashanti pulleys are often carved of dark wood and are drilled so that they may themselves be tied to the top beam. As befits the Ashanti passion for regalia and fetishes, these pulleys are often ornately carved to represent dolls, chiefly stools and heads. By contrast, the Ewe, despite a notoriety for the effective use of their particularly powerful form of juju, carve and use pulleys in the shape of birds, such as a cockerel and a hen; their beaks are sufficiently hooked to hang onto the top beam. Both groups see the pair of pulleys as male and female counterparts in the weaving process.

Once he has attached the warps securely to the cloth beam, the weaver is ready to create an even tension on the web by stretching the warps out flat from within a colourful and well-organized skein of yarn to a distance of between 10 and 40 feet (3 and 12 metres) from the loom structure. The warp skein then rests on a dragstone, which may take the form of a flat rock, a pile of rocks or a concrete block and which sits on a smooth sled, such as a plank of wood. The sled itself is attached to the warp threads, and the tension is created on the web by the link, which comprises a stick and clasp; thus the skein may be detached from the dragstone assembly with great ease and speed. Where the loom and the outstretched warps are not under cover, at the threat of rain, for example, the skein, heddles, pulleys, comb and cloth beam with completed textile may be removed within minutes; restoring the apparatus to continue the work is completed without fuss, and as the web of the weave is so narrow, it is relatively easy to restore the desired tension to the warps.

The experienced weaver is supported in his work by a number of apprentices and small boys, who adjust the length of the warp that is unravelled from the skein and dragstone, as well as operating the winders that charge the shuttles. The varying colours of yarn required for the weft inlays and for the weft itself are wound onto the bobbins ('dodowa'), ready for use within the shuttles ('kurokurowa' in Ashanti), by the weaver's assistants. The four-armed weft skein winder is known as a 'fwiridie', and from this rotating apparatus the thread is wound off onto the bobbins from within a winder similar to a toy sewing machine, known as a 'dadabena'. Not all the wefts are inserted by shuttles, for, as we have seen, certain small groups of inlay colours may be inserted by hand through the shed of the warps.

The background warp-faced weave is achieved by the weaver manipulating the *asatia* heddles in turn, using his feet, so that a shed is created, through which the shuttle containing the weft may be thrown from side to side in a blur of action that is coordinated with effortless ease. The *asanan* pedals will open the shed for the passage of the shuttle or hand insertion of the weft pattern inlay. From time to time the weave is evenly tamped down with the comb. So that there is an even spacing of the weft inlay blocks – if that is the desired effect – a measuring stick, the 'susudua', is laid parallel to the pattern in front of the weaver, enabling him to calculate the length of decorated work needed. The finished cloth is then rolled onto the cloth beam.

While the young boys and the apprentices are energetically learning the basics of the craft by adjusting the warp and winding the yarns, the elderly weavers look to work out their declining years patiently and skilfully sewing together the strips to create the finished wearing cloth. Sitting quietly, the older and retired weavers cut the finished cloth and hand-sew the strips together along their selvedges. The success of a composition depends on arranging the cut strips so that the sequence of patterns and colours of the inlay blocks within each strip is constantly varied across the whole width of the cloth. No amount of dexterous adjustment by an experienced old hand will, however, make up for poor alignment of the pattern blocks at the time of weaving. A 'fine' cloth, in which the pattern blocks are evenly spaced along the length of the warp, and therefore across the whole completed textile, can only be achieved by the diligence of the weaver.

It is quite obvious from the description of the Ashanti and Ewe strip-weaving process that the men and boys of the villages are the workers, and that women play no part in the activity. This is universally the case throughout the strip-weaving cultures of West Africa. Indeed, women are even excluded from the environs of the loom. Rattray makes much of this taboo amongst the Ashanti: 'Women could never be weavers owing to the fact that they have menstrual periods, said the chief of the [Bonwire] village. . . . A woman during her periods may not touch a loom. A woman in this condition must not even address her husband directly. . .'.

For the 'traditional' weaving cultures of West Africa weaving is seen as a god-given process, a manifest wonder of creativity, and the loom a divine instrument. Protective taboos have been refined over the centuries, therefore, to protect the apparatus and its creator from offensive spirits. Rattray observes, for instance: 'An old loom must on no account be burned or broken up; if it is broken accidentally, a fowl must be sacrificed upon it. A weaver who is going trading or on a journey will take up the parts of his loom and throw them into the river to prevent their ever being broken up for firewood.' In spite of the rapid social and cultural changes of a Westernized variety that have so perturbed the 'traditional' way of life and weakened the taboos, the act of strip-weaving continues to be an all-male preserve.

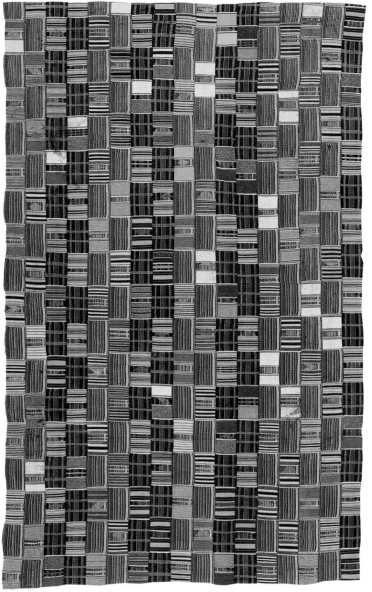

82

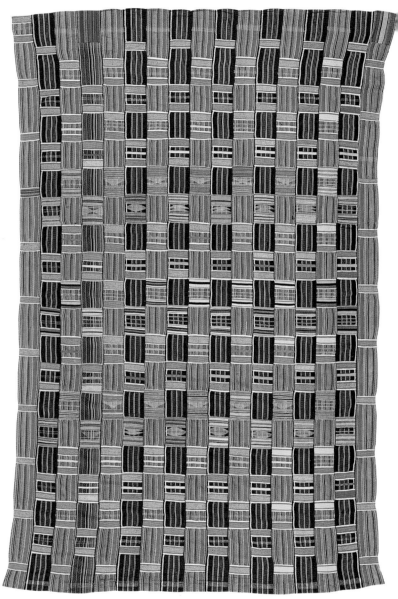

83

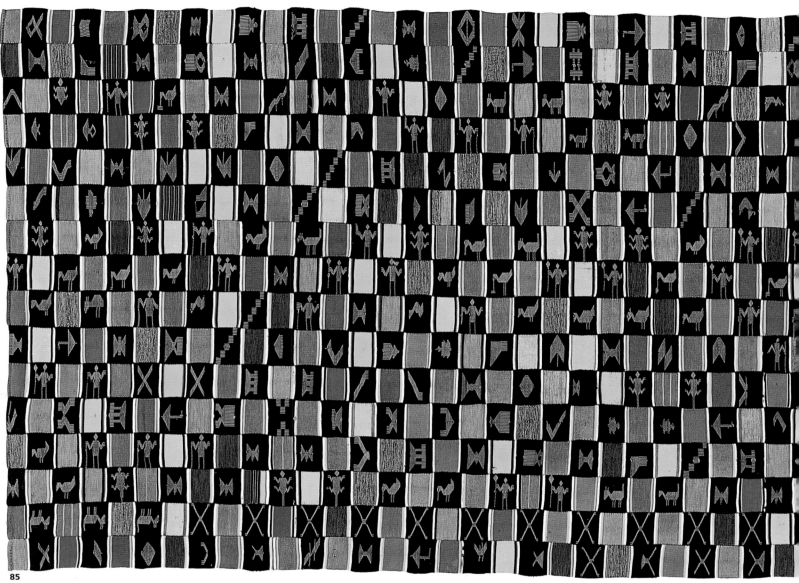

85

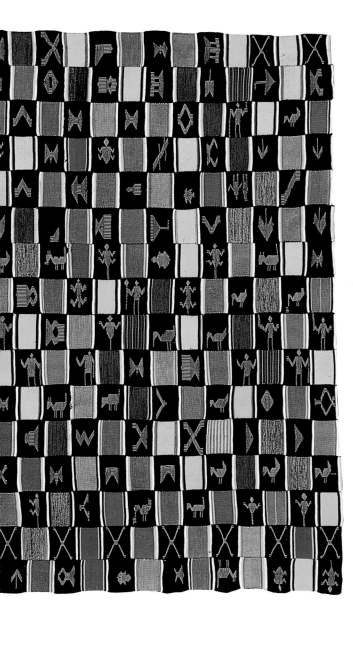

86

87

88 ▽

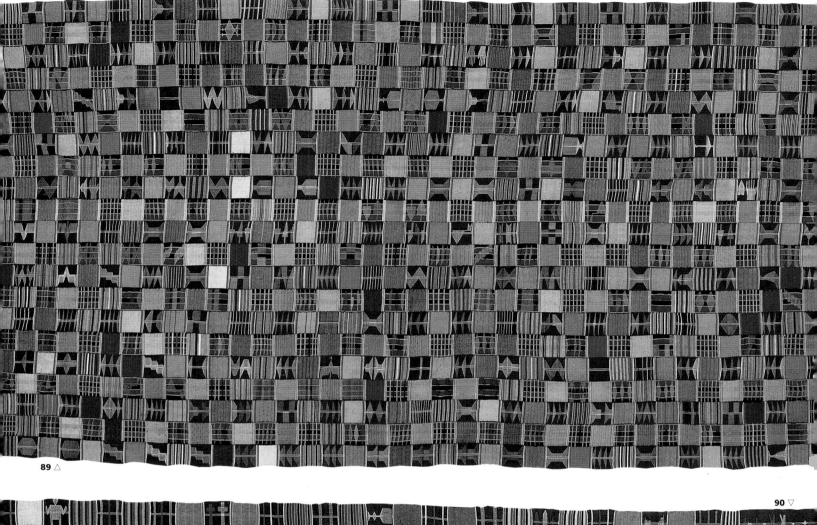

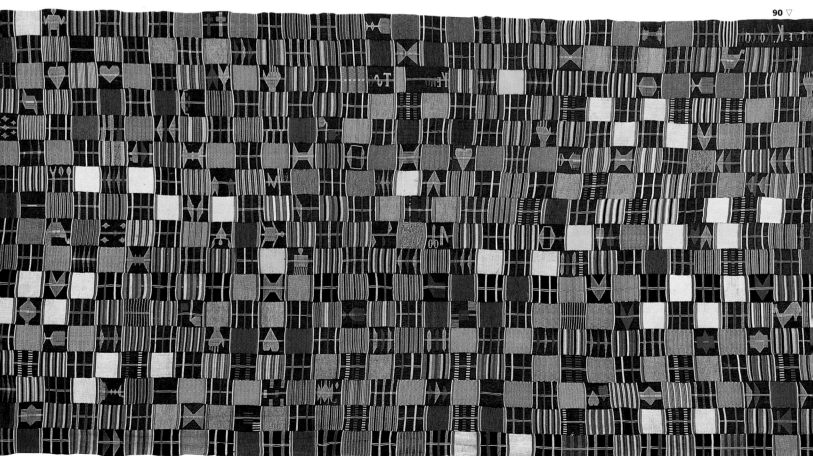

91

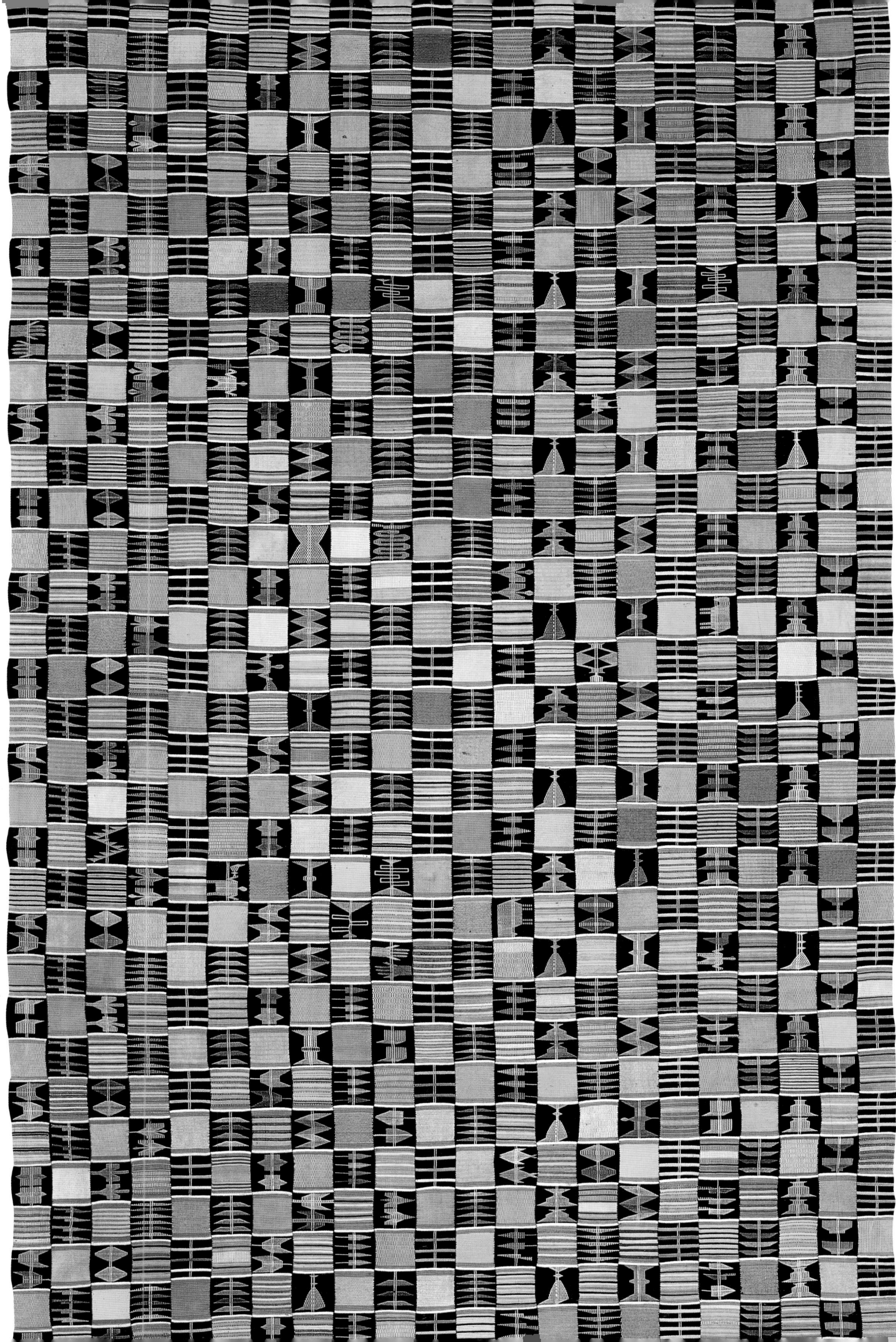

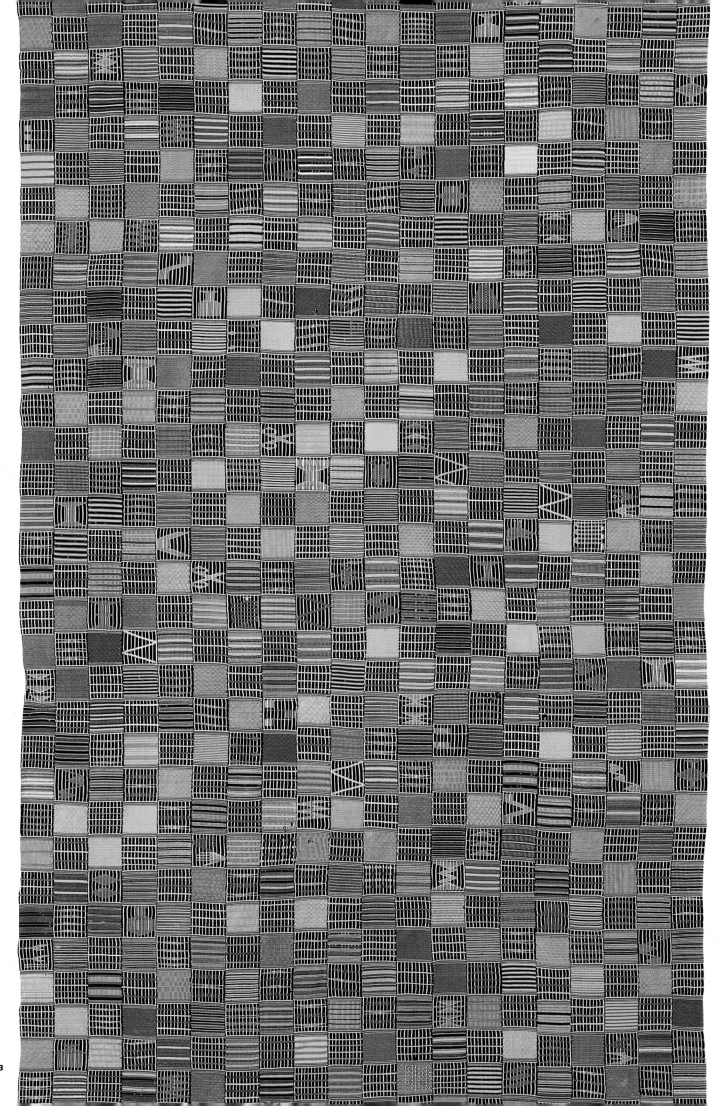

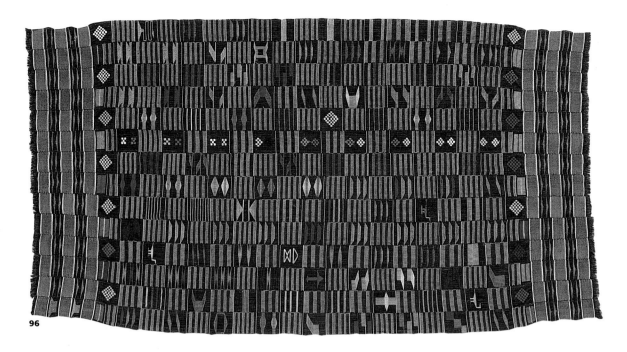

96

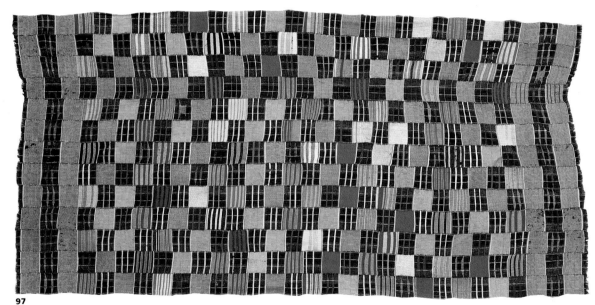

97

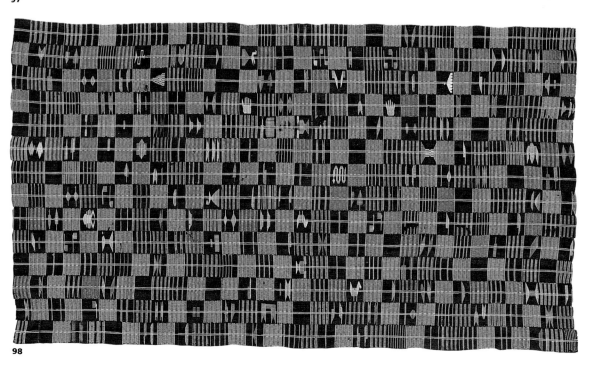

98

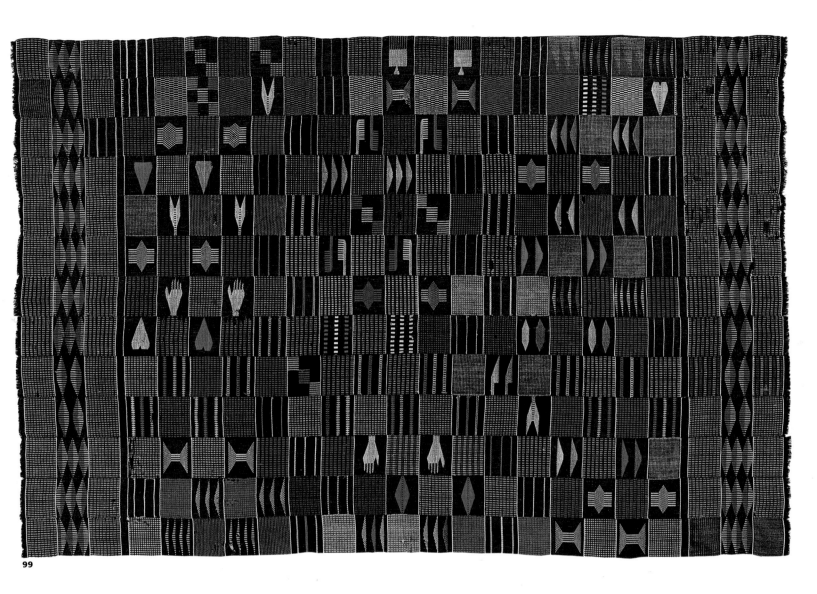

99

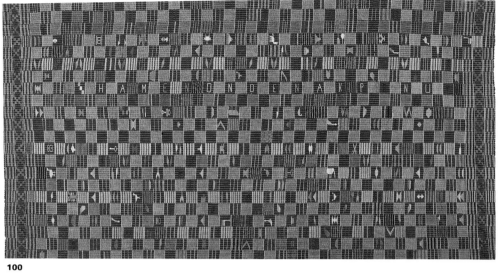

100

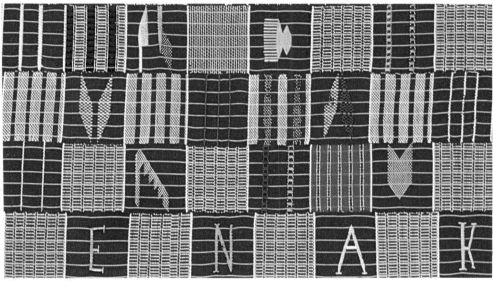

101

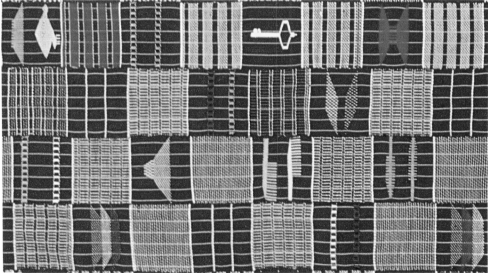

102

103

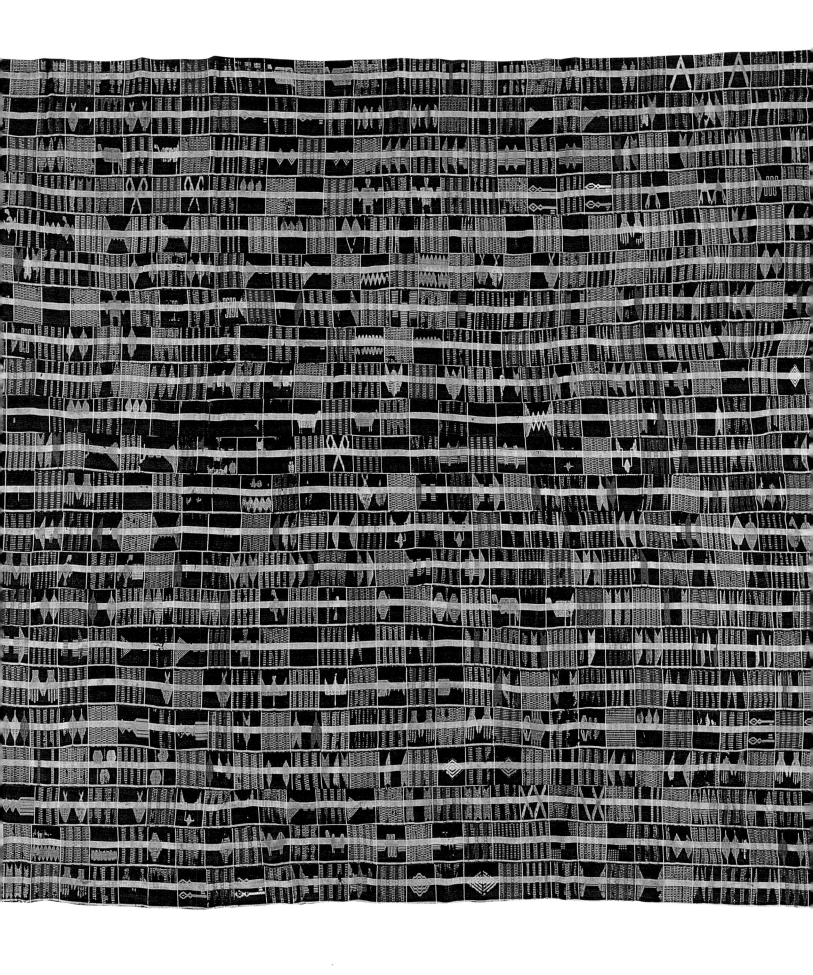

104

105

106

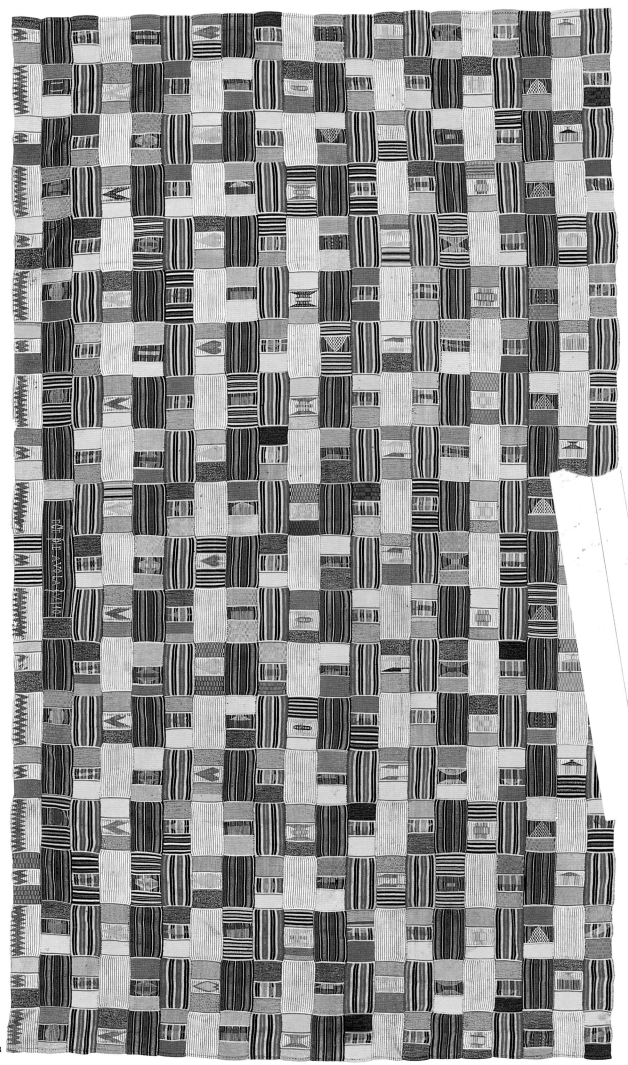

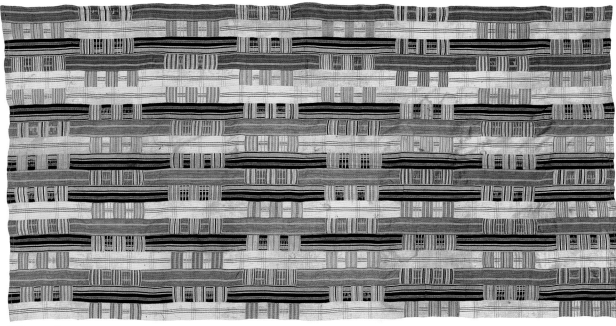

109

110

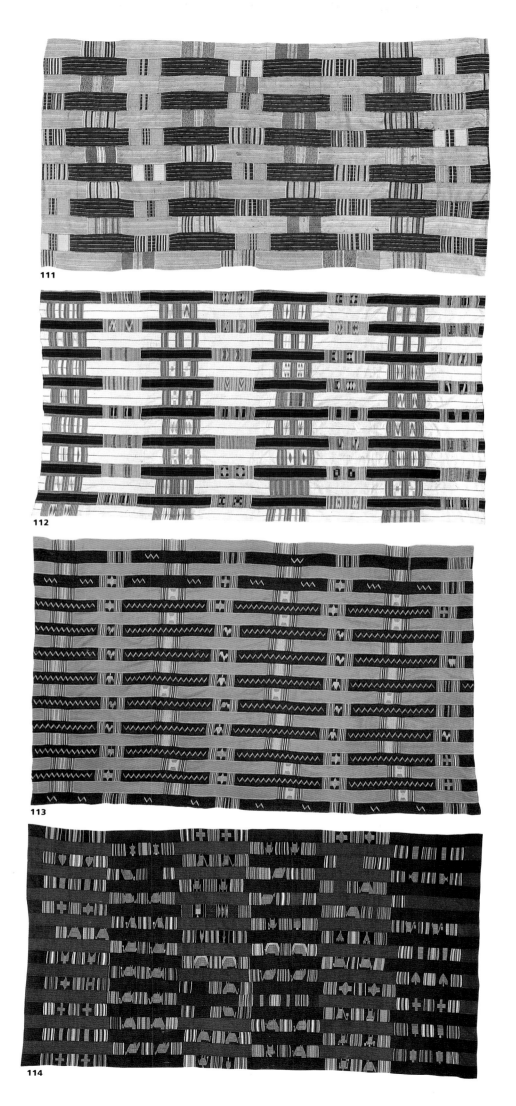

111

112

113

114

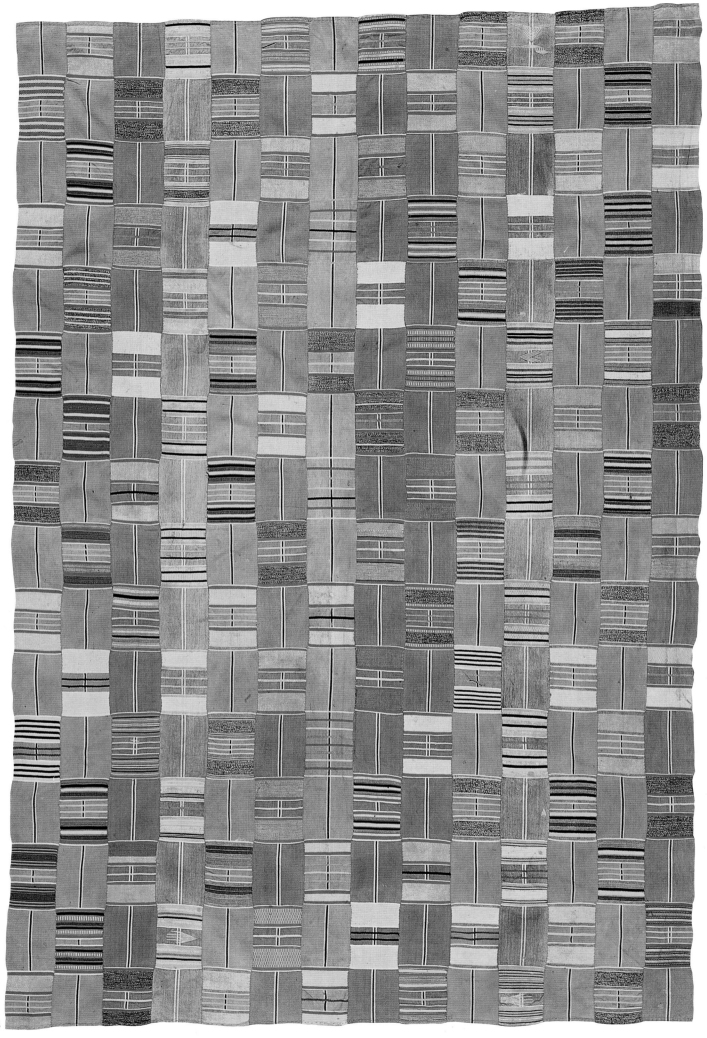

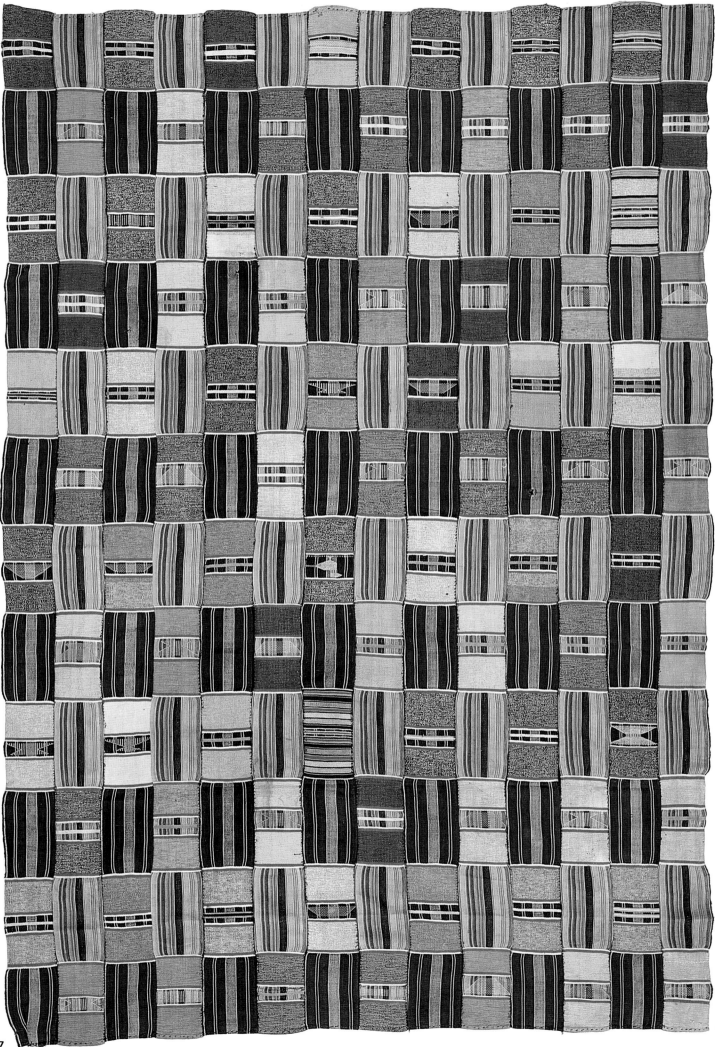

117

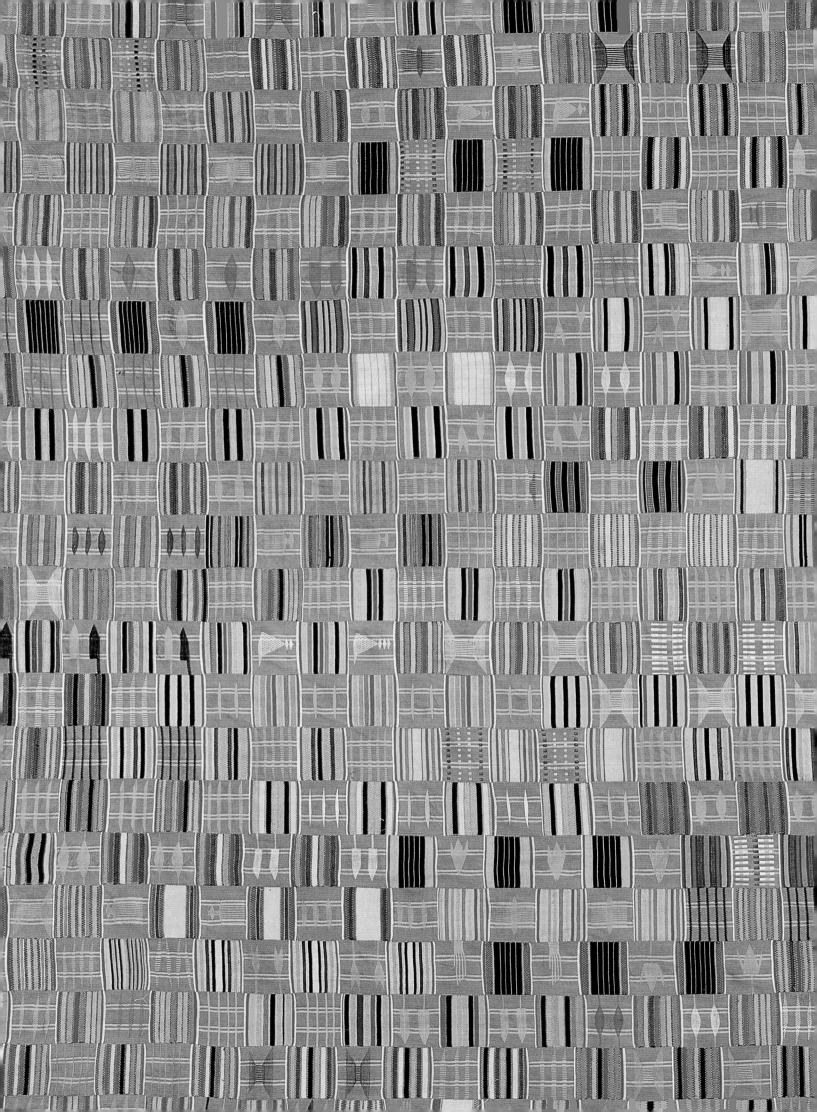

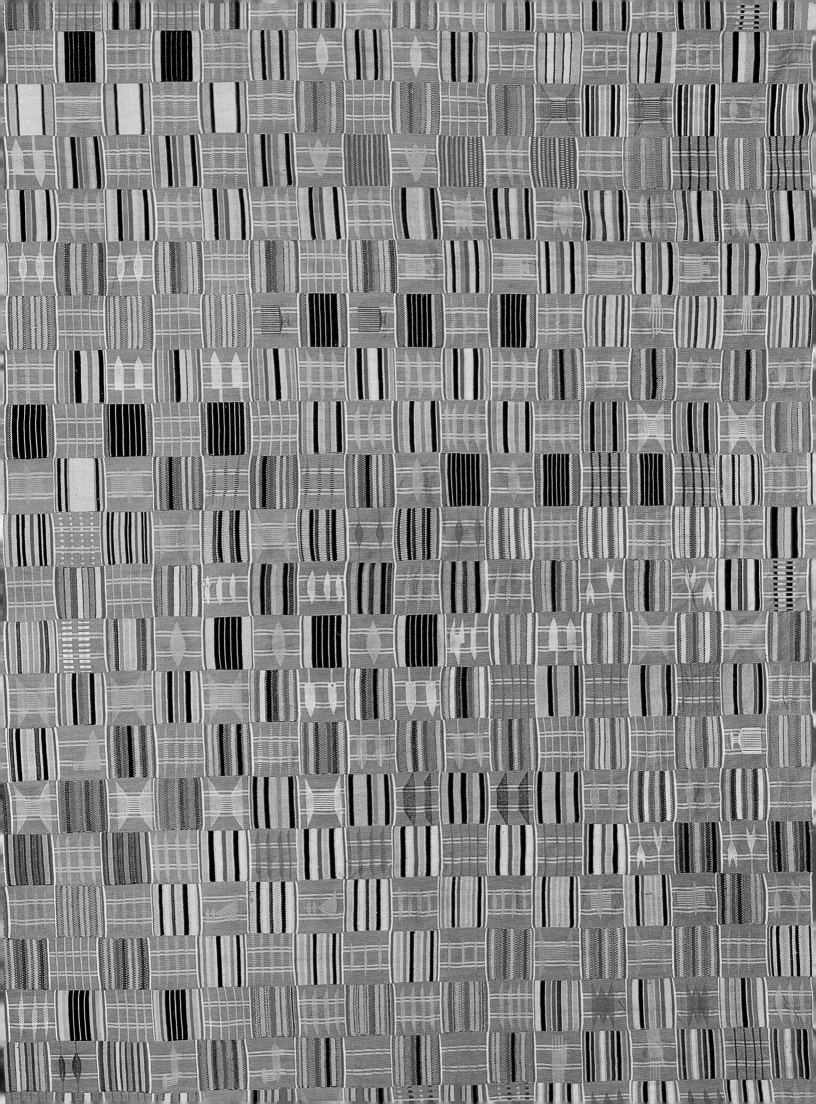

119

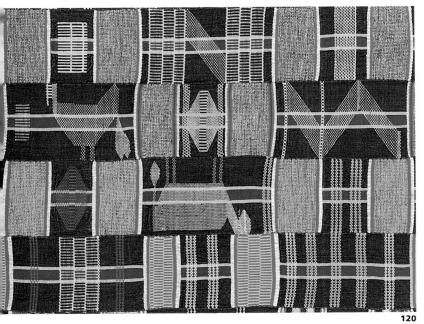

120

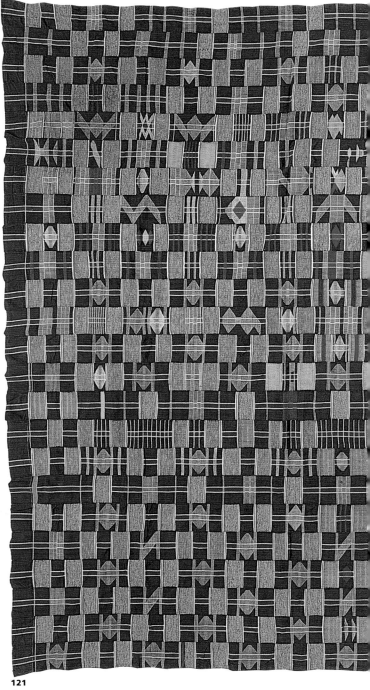

121

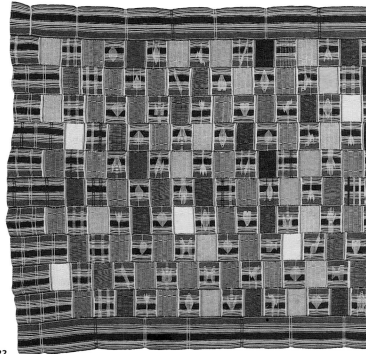

122

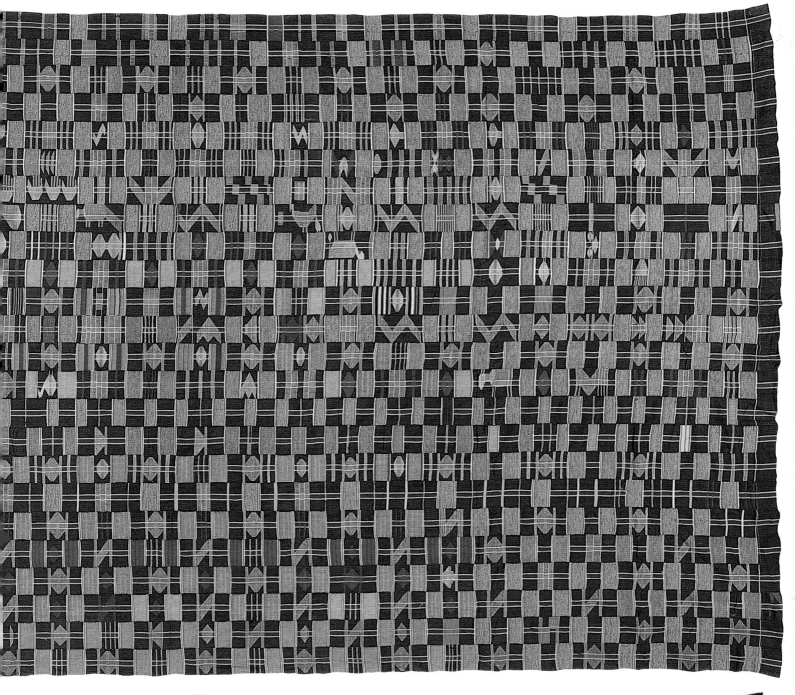

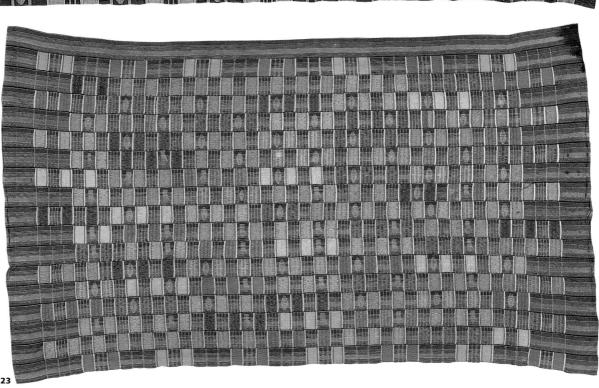

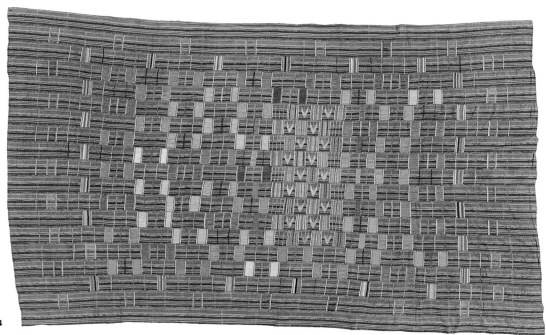

124

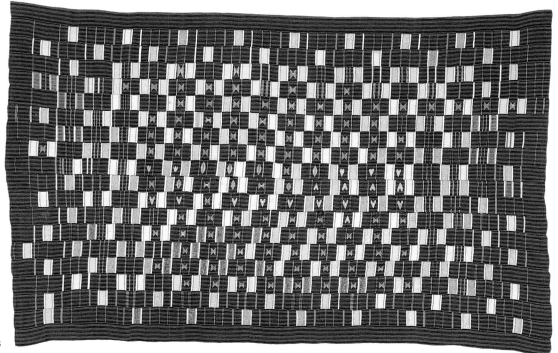

125

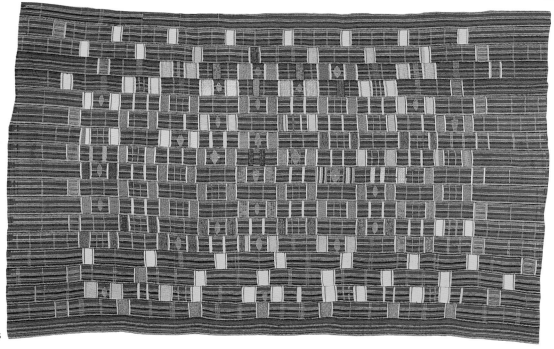

126

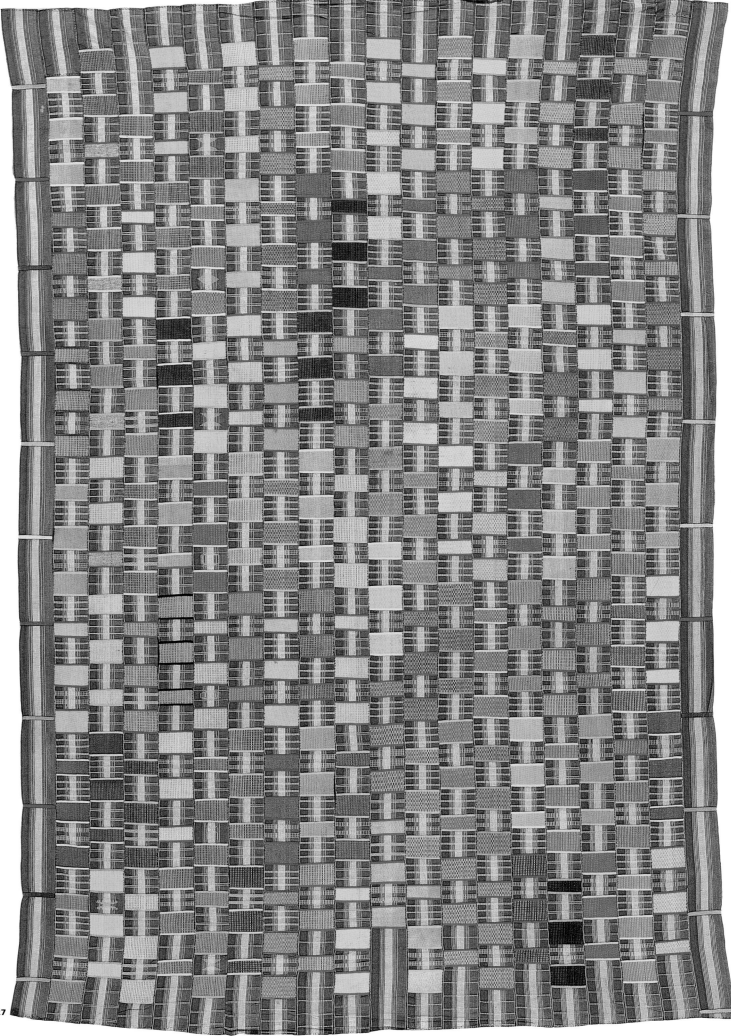

128

129

130

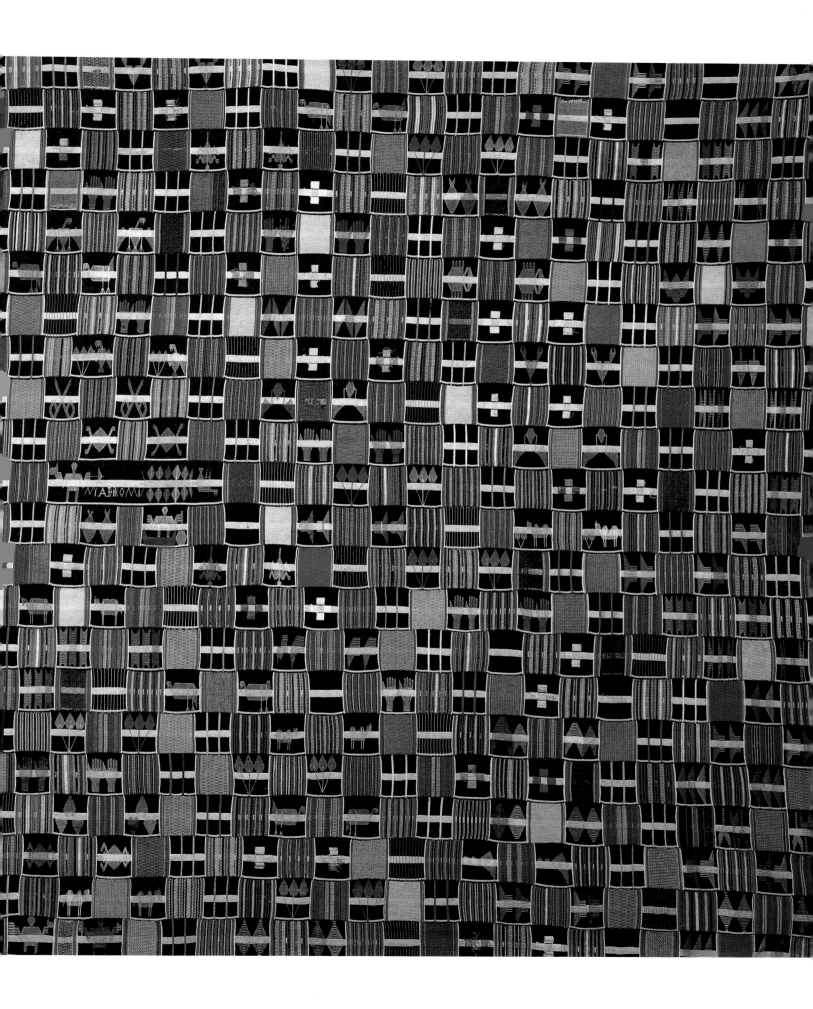

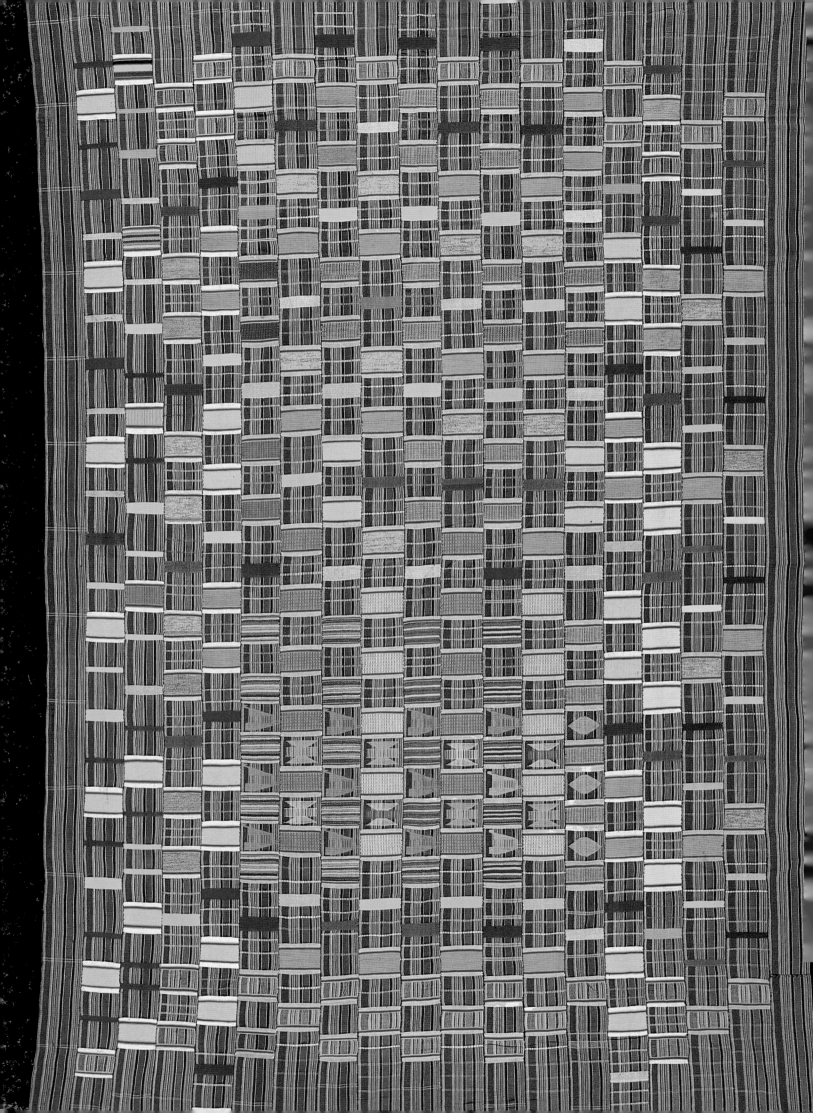

1

Type of cloth Ashanti man or woman's wrap
Local title of cloth Oyokoman Adweneasa Nsaduaso
Origin by tribe/group Ashanti
Place of origin Bonwire, Ghana
Type of yarn Silk warp and weft
Weaving techniques Plain weave with single and some double supplementary wefts
Number of strips 16
Overall size of cloth 138 × 200 cm

No section of this old silken cloth has been left without some form of exquisitely detailed extra weft patterning. The Ashanti describe such elaborate, time-consuming and painstaking work as 'Adweneasa', which was explained to me by an Ashanti weaver as meaning 'the end of all designs or skills in weaving. It is also known as the king of all designs.'

The background combination of red, yellow and green warp stripes is entitled *Oyokoman* (see plate 24, no. 29), and is associated with the finer weft-patterned cloths, such as Adweneasa and Asasia. Oyoko is the title of the royal clan of the Ashanti, and so in the past these colours were exclusively reserved for the chiefs.

Amidst the feast of patterns, the fine multi-coloured, but predominantly gold and black chequerboards were inspired by the staple foodstuffs of the weavers as one Ashanti weaver described it: 'corn and groundnuts. In most cases the weavers do their work with corn and groundnuts by their side and they will be eating the corn and groundnuts as they work.

There are instances when they are so busy with their work and they may not like to get up and eat.'

2

Type of cloth Ashanti woman's wrap
Local title of cloth Afurumu Aso N'toma
Origin by tribe/group Ashanti
Place of origin Ashanti region, Ghana
Type of yarn Cotton warp and weft
Weaving techniques Plain weave with single supplementary wefts
Number of strips 13
Overall size of cloth 109 × 173 cm

This small cloth may well have been worn by a wealthy Ashanti lady; the title of the chequered warp striping is less than flattering, however, for it translates as 'the ass's ear'. It was described thus: 'The cloth was used in festival days or durbar. It was worn only by those who were rich or big men who had a thousand pounds in the colonial days or its equivalent in gold. Therefore it was only prominent people in society who could put on this cloth.' R.S. Rattray describes the warp stripe in *Religion and Art in Ashanti* (1927) as follows (plate 4, no. 20): '*Afurumu aso* (the donkey's ear). This is a woman's cloth; it is an everyday dress and is chiefly worn for farm work.' Certainly, the Ashanti cotton cloths, all of which are blue and white, are associated with those outside the royal circle, or were sported by the chiefs as a sign of respect on ceremonial occasions.

3

Type of cloth Ashanti man's wrap
Local title of cloth Mmaban N'toma
Origin by tribe/group Ashanti
Place of origin Ashanti region
Type of yarn Cotton warp and weft
Weaving techniques Plain weave with supplementary wefts
Number of strips 16
Overall size of cloth 143 × 244 cm

The sewing together of strips of cloth with a variety of patterns creates a textile without a specific title; having no predominant warp pattern, this type of cloth is known as 'Mmaban', meaning mixed. Five different warp patterns are evident, and the following may be noted from Rattray's chart (plates 4 and 5). No. 20: '*Afurumu aso* (the donkey's ear).' No. 39: '*Kotwa* (the scar); also called *asambo* (the guinea-fowl's breast), and *asam'takra* (the guinea-fowl's feather). . . . Only worn by chiefs.' Such fine gingham check patterning has been found on some of the cloths discovered at the archaeological site of Bandiagara, which date from the eleventh century. Much trade cloth from south-eastern India is patterned in this style. No. 54: '*Aboadie. Aboadie* is perhaps synonymous with *Bosompra*, one of the *ntoro* patrilineal divisions; formerly worn by one of that division. This pattern is said to have been invented by Kwaku Dua I, for his children; at intervals are three white ribbed lines . . . and three blue lines (of the same width as those running up the warp) crossing the warp.'

Mmaban cloths such as this have a tremendous vitality and a quality of free expression in their composition; not only is there no regular and matching run of warp patterns, but the weft colour blocks do not line up across the textile either – a fine example for any textile designer of how the lack of a cohesive pattern repeat need not hinder the success of a cloth design.

4–5

These blue and white cotton samples and the succeeding coloured silks (plates 23–30) of the Ashanti were included by Rattray in his seminal work of 1927, *Religion and Art in Ashanti*. Rattray states: 'The expense of reproducing in colour samples large enough to show both the warp and the weft patterns is prohibitive, and I have had to be content in nearly every case to show only the warp samples, such as a weaver would himself mount before he commences to lay the warp; as already noted, it is from this that the textile derives its name. . . . I now propose to give the particulars I have been able to obtain concerning these designs. In each case the Ashanti name of the pattern will first be mentioned; and next the English equivalent of that name (where it is capable of explanation) will be given, with some additional information.'

1 *Boboserewa* (joy and sorrow), alternately called *Gyemeware* ('take me in marriage').
2 *Aduana*. The 'tartan' of the clan of that name.
3 *Krofa*. The derivation of this word is said to be *kodo*

(a wooden plate), and *fa* (half). In olden times only the King of Ashanti might wear this cloth.

4 *Akroma fufuo* (the white hawk).

5 *Ohene akamfo* (at the king's pleasure), also sometimes called *ohene nko nyon* or *ohene nko mfura*, 'the king only may weave', or 'the king only may wear'; said to have been personally designed by King Kwaku Dua I (A D 1838).

6 *Hiampoa* ('I lack even a penny'). The poor man's cloth.

7 *Asebi Hene* (the Asebi chief). He was in charge of the King of Ashanti's weavers; and it was worn by the chief of that stool, or by others with the king's permission. [For the weft pattern see plate 5, no. 69.]

8 *Kyere 'Twie* (catch the leopard). This is said to refer to an incident during the reign of King Kwaku Dua I, when that monarch ordered some Ashanti to catch a leopard alive.

9 *Akoko de boro be kum ako* ('the fowl may beat the parrot until it kills it').

10 *Antoko* ('they did not meet the enemy'). Said to refer to an historical event in the reign of Bonsu Panyin, when Amankwatia, the Ashanti general, was sent to reinforce the army already in the field, but before he arrived the campaign was over. It was worn by the Ashanti general and the King of the Ashanti.

11 *Krofa Nsafoa*. [Variation on no. 3.]

12 *Nyawoho* (*Nkyimkyim*) ('he has become rich'); *nkyimkyim* means bent, crooked, and refers to the design at intervals on the weft (see no. 72). It is stated that in olden times a man had to be worth £1,000, in gold dust, to wear this pattern, with the king's permission.

13 *Tetewara koro* (the single small strip cloth). This refers to the blue line running up the side of the warp. The word *tetewa* is used by the weavers to designate any remains of yarn left over after weaving a cloth, *tete* (old), *wa* (the diminutive).

14 *Nnapane* (sleep alone); a bachelor is said to *da pane* (sleep alone). The King of Ashanti might not wear this pattern unless at a funeral and when dyed with red clay.

15 *Nkatewasa* ('the *nkatewa* seeds have come to an end').

16 *Biribi ne hia nse* ('there is nothing so bad as poverty'). A poor man's cloth.

17 *'Fodua* (the colobus monkey's tail).

18 *Tentene*. Called after a worm of that name.

19 *Akroma* (the hawk).

20 *Afurumu aso* (the donkey's ear). This is a woman's cloth; it is an everyday dress and is chiefly worn for farm work.

21 *Anene kom'* (round the crow's neck).

22 *Asikyiri ne Burowo* (sugar and honey). Worn by the Queen Mothers and chiefs.

23 *Makowa* (the little pepper).

24 *Ademkyemyamu* (inside the belly of the crocodile). Formerly worn only by chiefs and sub-chiefs.

25 *Adjai Bohyen*. Called after a Bonwere [*sic*] weaver of that name who lived in ancient times.

26 *Aburo ahahan* (corn leaves). Worn by the paramount chiefs.

27 *Mosi Nkoasa* (the three Mosi slaves).

28 *Nsankani tuntum* (the black nsankani flower).

Formerly only worn by the King of Ashanti and *Amanhene* [paramount chiefs].

29 *Damienu* ('the two who rest side by side').

30 *Se die fofoo pe, ne se gyinantwi abo bedie* ('What the yellow-flowered *fofoo* plant wants is that the *gyinantwi* seeds should turn black'). This is a well-known Ashanti saying. The *fofoo*, the botanical name of which is *Bidens pilosa*, has a small yellow flower, which, when it drops its petals, turns into a black spiky seed. Said of a jealous person. Some Ashanti know this pattern under the name of *Akurase* (the teeth of the mouse).

31 *Asikyiri ne Burowo Tuntum* [black or dark sugar and honey; see no. 22.]

32 *Higya* (the lion). The Bonwere weavers told me this design is not correct and was never one of the old-established patterns.

33 *Wa yi me bako* ('I am the one to be driven out'). This design would appear to be of doubtful origin, as it was unknown to the older Bonwere weavers.

34 *Nkasawesewa* (the clever orator); formerly worn by Queen Mothers.

35 *Bewo.* Called after a princess of the *Oyoko* clan who married the chief of Tafo during the reign of Osai Tutu.

36 *Nsafoasia* (the six keys); formerly worn by the king's treasurers.

37 *Adwire Nkyemu* (the squirrel's flank); it might be worn by a freeman.

38 *Agyinegyeninsu.* The name of a black water insect.

39 *Kotwa* (the scar); also called *asambo* (the guinea-fowl's breast), and *asam'takra* (the guinea-fowl's feather). . . . Only worn by chiefs.

40 *Ekomenmu* (between the buffalo's horns).

41 *Ahene mma mfura* ('let the king's children wear it'). Said to have been designed by King Kwaku Dua I for his children.

42 *Akagya* (a kind of squirrel).

43 *Etesiwani* (a white spot in the pupil of the eye).

44 *Ahene mma ntama* (the cloth of the king's children).

5

45 *Abusua fwidie gu nkorowa* (separate clans fall into groups(?)).

46 *Onyina ne no man* (the silk-cotton tree and its branches).

47 *Abusuasa* (the three clans).

48 *Nsafoasa* (the three keys). See number 70 for the weft pattern, at intervals.

49 *Nkruma 'Kwan* (the paths leading to the *okro* farm). A woman's cloth, formerly worn only by the Queen Mothers and princesses.

50 *Adopie Konmu* (the fairies' neck).

51 *Asomorodwe Mpampamu* (the crown of the *asomorodwe* beetle's head). The Bonwere weavers stated that there is a slight error in the design.

52 *Nnapane nketewa* (the lesser *nnapane* pattern). See number 14.

53 *Nankatiri* (the puff-adder's head). Worn only by men, because '*nankatiri ye twa no 'barima na yentwa no ba*' ('a man, not a woman, cuts off the *nankatiri*'s head').

54 *Aboadie. Aboadie* is perhaps synonymous with

Bosompra, one of the *ntoro* patrilineal divisions; formerly worn by one of that division. This pattern is said to have been invented by Kwaku Dua I, for his children.

55 *Yiwa ne bota* (the Yiwa and Bota beads). Formerly only worn by the King of Ashanti.

56 *Kyekye*; lit. hard, stiff, so-called from the ribbed effect in the weft.

57 *Damienu*. See number 29. This pattern, I was informed, is symbolical of the two stools of Coomassie and Mampon, the Golden Stool and the Silver Stool.

58 *Ahenemma nsafoa* (the keys of the king's children).

59 *Fwintea* (the seed of a tree?).

60 *Matatwine*. The name of a creeping plant, which is also medicinal; there is a saying which runs: '*Ofuntum wuo esane matatwine*', 'When the *ofuntum* tree dies, the *matatwine* (which entwines it) also dies (relaxes its hold)'.

61 *Ntontom beforo 'po?* ('Does a mosquito cross the sea?').

62 *Panpana ahanan* (Panpana leaves).

63 *Mosi*. Name of a tribe, supposed to represent their tribal markings.

64 *Nankatiri*. Compare number 53, the same design, with a somewhat narrower blue warp.

65 *Okomfo Akua* (the Priestess Akua).

66 *Afe* (the comb), see number 71 for weft pattern, at intervals.

67 *Ennamenkoso* ('the fault is not mine').

68 *Nsafoatonton* (the big keys, worn by the king's treasurers).

69 *Asebi Hene*, see number 7.

70 *Nsafoa*. See also number 48.

71 *Afe*. See also number 66.

72 *Nyawoho*. See number 12.

6

Type of cloth Ashanti man's cloth
Local title of cloth Esoro Akyempim N'toma
Origin by tribe/group Ashanti
Place of origin Bonwire, Ghana
Type of yarn Silk warp and weft
Weaving techniques Plain weave with single and double supplementary wefts
Number of strips 24
Overall size of cloth 185 × 305 cm

Rattray notes this type of cloth in number 31 of his silk colour swatches (plate 24) as: '*Akyempim* ("he has given him one thousand"). Tradition states that this design dates from the reign of Osai Tutu (1700), and owes its origin to a gift from that monarch to one Owusu Efiriye, the Akyempim chief. The warp pattern has upon it at intervals parallelograms woven in yellow and maroon.' Here Rattray is confusing the warp pattern with the overall 'title' of the cloth. The warp pattern, according to B. Menzel, is entitled *Esoro*. The arrangement of the tiny inlay blocks of colour explains why the cloth is known by the appropriate title of *Akyempim*, which means 'one thousand shields', implying that the bearer knows no fear. Such a well-defined and spacious mosaic and terrazzo composition within the field of the cloth is highly unusual for West African strip-weaves. The densely woven borders provide a striking framework, alternating between the *wotoa* weft inlay blocks of red and yellow checks, the blocks of bands of colour, and the 'unity is strength' pattern, divided into two colours, entitled *Abusua ye dem tabono*; *tabono*, *ntabon* or *tabombma* means paddle.

7

Type of cloth Ashanti man's cloth
Local title of cloth Mmaban N'toma
Origin by tribe/group Ashanti
Place of origin Ashanti region
Type of yarn Cotton warp and weft
Weaving techniques Plain weave with single and double supplementary wefts
Number of strips 24
Overall size of cloth 206 × 323 cm

In contrast to the majority of cotton blue and white Ashanti cloths, this large textile, which is made up of strips of mixed warp patterning, is predominantly blue in tone. The white supplementary inlays break up the composition, creating an element of irregularity that makes the viewer's gaze shift constantly between the desire for order and delight in the abstract variations. Warp patterns and weft characteristics noted by Rattray include number 20 (plate 4): *Afurumu aso* (the donkey's ear); number 24 (plate 4): *Ademkyemyamu* (inside the belly of the crocodile); number 36 (plate 4): the reverse in colours of *Nsafoasia* (the six keys); and number 56 (plate 5); *Kyekye*, meaning stiff, from the ribbed effect of the weft.

8

Type of cloth Ashanti man's cloth
Local title of cloth Mmeda Apampam Nsaduaso
Origin by tribe/group Ashanti
Place of origin Bonwire, Ghana
Type of yarn Silk warp and weft
Weaving techniques Plain weave with single and double supplementary wefts
Number of strips 23
Overall size of cloth 206 × 320 cm

The four-part border pattern of this unevenly woven cloth is known as *Abusua ye dem nsatea*. A weaver explained: 'That is, "unity is strength"; *nsatea* means fingers. We have various "unity is strength" and this particular one is known as finger type of "unity is strength".' Within the field is the single appearance of an unusually refined (*atwere*) ladder pattern.

9

Type of cloth Ashanti woman's cloth
Local title of cloth Mmeeda peemu Nsaduaso
Origin by tribe/group Ashanti
Place of origin Bonwire, Ghana
Type of yarn Silk warp and weft
Weaving techniques Plain weave with single and double supplementary wefts
Number of strips 14
Overall size of cloth 120 × 173 cm

The border of this cloth shows the popular pattern 'unity is strength with fisherman's paddle'.

10

Type of cloth Ashanti man's cloth
Local title of cloth Asambo Nsaduaso
Origin by tribe/group Ashanti
Place of origin Bonwire, Ghana
Type of yarn Silk warp and weft
Weaving techniques Plain weave with single and
double supplementary wefts
Number of strips 22
Overall size of cloth 182 × 300 cm

The warp pattern of this cloth was described as
follows: 'This is known as *Asambo*, that is the guinea-
fowl's chest. If you have seen this bird or fowl you will
observe that the feather designs are the same as the
background of this cloth. The end is "unity is strength
with fisherman's paddle" (*Abusua ye dem tabono*).'
Rattray describes this warp pattern (plate 24, no. 43)
as '*Asambo* (the breast of the guinea-fowl), sometimes
also called *asam 'takra* (the guinea-fowl's feather), and
sometimes *Kotwa* (a scar).'

This cloth shows very clearly the exact alternation
and regular linking of the pattern blocks in relation to
the background pattern, a technique known as *susudua*
(see p. 61).

11

Type of cloth Ashanti man's cloth
Local title of cloth Mmaban N'toma
Origin by tribe/group Ashanti
Place of origin Bonwire, Ghana
Type of yarn Silk warp and weft

Weaving techniques Plain weave with single and
double supplementary wefts
Number of strips 24
Overall size of cloth 195 × 316 cm

'This cloth is known as *Mmaban N'toma*. It means
mixture of cloths. Here the weaver, after weaving so
many cloths, may have some pieces which are excesses
of various cloths, and when such excesses are put
together it becomes mixture of cloths which have not
got any particular name.' Warp patterns seen here
include *Oyokoman* (plate 24, no. 29), *Asonawo mmada*
(plate 25, no. 53) and *Hoaasonawo* (plate 23, no. 19).

12

Type of cloth Ashanti man's cloth
Local title of cloth Mmaban N'toma
Origin by tribe/group Ashanti
Place of origin Bonwire, Ghana
Type of yarn Silk warp and weft
Weaving techniques Plain weave with single and
double supplementary wefts
Number of strips 22
Overall size of cloth 190 × 280 cm

Here again the strips of cloth do not match, and so, by
Ashanti values, this is not a 'fine' cloth. To Western
eyes, though, the wonder lies in its visual vigour.

13

Type of cloth Ashanti man's cloth
Local title of cloth Mmaban N'toma

Origin by tribe/group Ashanti
Place of origin Bonwire, Ghana
Type of yarn Silk warp and weft
Weaving techniques Plain weave with single and double supplementary wefts
Number of strips 23
Overall size of cloth 179 × 320 cm

The ingenious relationship between weft inlays and the warp striping is quite remarkable within the field of this 'mixed' cloth. At times the inlays are of double weave and obscure the warps. There are motifs, such as crosses, that have been enhanced by the sudden appearance of a segment of the warp colours, while large bands of bright, undecorated areas provide a striking contrast to the intense patterning. Designs include: *nkyinkyim*, the electric zig-zag; *trom nwoma*, a representation of a chequerboard; as well as the familiar fisherman's paddle with 'unity is strength', *Abusua ye dem tabono*.

14–16
Details of plate 13

17
Type of cloth Ashanti man's cloth
Local title of cloth Oyokoman Nsaduaso
Origin by tribe/group Ashanti
Place of origin Bonwire, Ghana
Type of yarn Silk warp and weft
Weaving techniques Plain weave with single and double supplementary wefts

Number of strips 18
Overall size of cloth 146 × 315 cm

The narrowness of this old *Oyokoman* man's cloth is due to the fact that some of its strips have been damaged and removed. There is tremendous subtlety in the arrangement of the *susudua*, through the use of both single (Topreko) and double (Faprenu) weaves. The border fringe of zig-zags was described as '*Kesan*, meaning "if one travels, one should try to come back home, for home is home". Especially, when it is well with him, he should not remain in the foreign land; he should try to develop his roots.' Menzel notes this pattern as *nkyinkyim*, the electric zig-zag. The double diamond design is known as *nankatiri*, head of the Gabon viper, and the quadruple arrow flèches are entitled *mmodwewa*.

18–20
Details of plate 17

21
Type of cloth Ashanti man's cloth
Local title of cloth Asona Nsaduaso
Origin by tribe/group Ashanti
Place of origin Bonwire, Ghana
Type of yarn Silk warp and weft
Weaving techniques Plain weave with single and double supplementary wefts
Number of strips 25
Overall size of cloth 216 × 322 cm

This pattern seems to be a green variation on Rattray's number 53, (plate 25), *Asonawo mmada*: 'The clan "tartan" of the Asona tribe'. The interpretation from Ghana supports this: 'The cloth is known as *Mmeda Asona Ahahamono. Mmeda* means "we have never seen some before". This is related to the beauty of the cloth. The cloth is so beautiful they have never seen such a cloth in their life-time. *Asona* is a clan in Akan ethnic group in Ghana, and *Ahahamono* means the fresh green leaf. The design at the fringe of the cloth is named in our language as *Suro Nipa*, meaning "fear your fellow human being, particularly the person very close to you".' Menzel lists this warp pattern as *apopobibire* (green) *mmeeda* (something unusual, a new creation) and the fringe pattern as *nkyemfre* (pieces, segments, fragments).

22

Type of cloth Ashanti man's cloth
Local title of cloth Nkontompa Nsaduaso
Origin by tribe/group Ashanti
Place of origin Bonwire, Ghana
Type of yarn Silk warp and weft
Weaving techniques Plain weave with single and double supplementary wefts
Number of strips 20
Overall size of cloth 161 × 286 cm

This is the well-known warp-patterned cloth, in an unusual colour, which Rattray describes in number 95 (plate 27) as *Nkontompo ntama* (the liar's cloth): 'The King of Ashanti is said to have worn this pattern when holding court, to confute persons of doubtful veracity who came before him.' In Ghana the following observation was made: '*Nkontompo N'toma*: it means in Ashanti language as "liar's cloth". This can be interpreted as meaning that the weaver of the cloth is lazy and not frank. According to the history behind the cloth, the weaver told the buyer that he was going to make him a very fine and complex cloth, but he came out with such a simple cloth of low value.' The mismatching centre is most probably the result of damage; strips have been removed, and the cloth sewn back together, albeit in the incorrect sequence.

23

These examples of Ashanti silk designs are taken from R.S. Rattray's *Religion and Art in Ashanti* (1927). Rattray gives the following explanations for their titles:

1 *Adjua Afwefwe* (beautiful Adjua), a girl's name, probably called after some beauty of ancient days. Bowdich records a similar naming of a cloth after a woman: He writes: '. . . The beautiful Adumissa is still eulogized and her favourite patterned cloth bears her name among the natives.'
2 *Sama.* Called after a man of that name, the son of one of the former chiefs at Bonwere, the village of the weavers.
3 Known as *kyemfere* (the potsherd), or sometimes *ponko se* (the horse's tooth).
4 *Otromo* (the Bongo).
5 *Tweneboa*, also sometimes called *Ntokosie*; the

former is the name of a woman whom tradition states to have been the wife of one Pampa, who was a weaver to one of the old-time Ashanti kings. This cloth might only be worn by the Kings of Ashanti; the meaning of the latter name is obscure.

6 *Kofi Esono* (Kofi, the Elephant), an Ashanti celebrity who was presented with this cloth by the King of Ashanti and given permission to wear it.

7 *Atabia Bene*, probably a person's name.

8 *Ofebiriti*. A 'strong name', *mmerane*, of King Kakari; might only be worn by the king.

9 *Atabia* (the name of a small antelope).

10 *Kwakye Asare*. Called after a prince of the Asona clan.

11 *Amere* (a personal name), formerly only worn by the King of Ashanti.

12 *Abawere* (the name of a small bird), 'the Queen Mother of all birds' (*anoma nhyina 'ni abawere*). Yaa Akyaa, Queen Mother of Ashanti, used to wear this pattern of cloth. Worn by Queen Mothers.

13 *Bansoa* (the name of a small white, black, and yellow bird; said to be very brave). There is a saying *Bansoa di 'ben* (the Bansoa bird eats the arrow).

14 *Dokoasiri Krofa*; exact meaning obscure. Formerly worn only by the King of Ashanti.

The weft design at intervals on this warp is very striking; it may be seen in [plate 30] no. 108.

15 *Ansaku*, a former King of Akwamu.

16 *Nkwantia ogye akore* ('It is at the small crossroads that the sacrifice is pegged down'); relation to design obscure.

17 *Ntumedie* (flying sparks from a bush fire); the

Bonwere weavers, however, state it is in the Ntokosie designs called *Kwame Badie*, a personal name; 'the white is the ash, the crimson, the sparks, and black, the burned grass.'

18 *Atoko* (lit. 'they met the enemy').

19 *Abusuakuruwa* (the clan's pot); the Bonwere weavers, however, call this design *Hoaasonawo* (the blue *asona* snake).

20 *Adweneasa*. This word means literally 'my skill is exhausted'; or 'my ideas have come to an end'. This pattern is one of the best known in Ashanti, and weavers who can make it are considered masters of their craft. In olden times only the Kings of Ashanti might wear this pattern. One of the cloths presented by the Ashanti to the Princess Mary on the occasion of her wedding was of this design.

21 *Nkuruma Bete* (the soft *okro*). *Hibiscus esculentus*, much used by the West African in soups.

22 *Dokoasiri*, or *Nokoasiri*; derivation obscure; several designs, varying slightly in detail, are all classed under this title (e.g. see [plate 24] no. 26). In olden days this pattern might only be worn by the King or Queen Mother of Ashanti.

24

R.S. Rattray's silk colour swatches continued:

23 *Ohene Akamfuo* ((it has) the king's approbation); in olden times might only be worn by the King of Ashanti, or by others with his permission.

24 *Makowa* (the little pepper), so called from the design woven at intervals to represent red and yellow

peppers. Lesser chiefs might wear this pattern.

25 *Asase ne abuo* (lit. the earth and its rocks); there is also a plant so named; the association of the name with this design is obscure. This design might be worn by chiefs.

26 Another of the *Dokoasiri* designs.

27 *Bese Hene* (the king of the kola-nuts); the white kola-nut is so called.

28 *Abodaban* (the iron bars of the castle); the Bonwere weavers, however, class this pattern among the *Dokoasiri*. This cloth in olden times might only be worn among the *amanhene* (paramount chiefs).

29 *Oyokoman ogya da mu* ('there is fire between the two factions of the *Oyoko* clan'); referring to the civil war after the death of Osai Tutu between Opoku Ware and the Dako. This cloth was worn by the King of Ashanti at the Kwesi Adae (Sunday Adae ceremony). It is the clan 'tartan' of the Royal House.

30 *Ntumoa* (the sand flies); also sometimes called *Srafo biri* (the black army); only worn by the *Amanhene* (paramount chiefs).

31 *Akyempim* ('he has given him one thousand'). Tradition states that this design dates from the reign of Osai Tutu (1700), and owes its origin to a gift from that monarch to one Owusu Efiriye, the Akyempim chief. The warp pattern has upon it at intervals parallelograms woven in yellow and maroon.

32 *Toku ne 'Kra tama* (the soul cloth of the Queen Mother Toku). Toku is reported to have been a Queen whom the Ashanti king Opoku Ware overthrew and killed; he took from her a cloth of this pattern, which he gave to the Queen Mother of Ashanti. Formerly

only worn by the Queen Mother of Ashanti.

33 *Kyirebin* (called after a deadly snake of that name; one of the titles of the Ashanti kings). The weavers at Bonwere call this pattern *Semea*.

34 *Kyime Kyerewere* or *Kyime Ahahamono* (*Kyime* who seizes and devours, or the green *Kyime* cloth). The loin-cloths of Kings and Queens of Ashanti were made in this pattern. There are no weft designs in this cloth.

35 *Nkateaasa birie* ('the black *nkwtewa* seeds are finished'). There is not any doubt but that some historical allusion, which I have been unable to trace, survives in this name. The pattern was formerly only worn by the Ashanti kings.

36 *Oyoko ne Dako* (the *Oyoko* and *Dako* clans).

37 *Afua Sapon* (the name of a Queen Mother in the reign of Agyeman I). Worn by Queen Mothers at the Wukudae ceremony.

38 *Aberewaben*. Aberewaben was a woman of the Asenie clan who lived in the time of Kwabia Amanfi (about AD 1600). This cloth used to be worn by the Adonten chief (leader of centre of Ashanti army).

39 *Ko'ntiri ne Akwamu*. This design might be worn by the Asafo, Adum and Bantama chiefs.

40 *Firimpoma*. Firimpoma was Queen Mother of Bonwere and grandmother of Ota Kraban, the first weaver. Formerly worn by Queen Mothers of Bonwere.

41 *Mmada K'rofa*. The meaning of this name is obscure. There was a room in the palace of the Ashanti kings known as *Mmada*, in which after the new king had been enstooled he was compelled to

sleep for seven nights, after which he was never to sleep there again as long as he lived; the room would not again be slept in until his successor came to be enstooled.

42 *Nyankonton* (the Sky God's arch), the rainbow; might only be worn with the permission of the king.

43 *Asambo* (the breast of the guinea-fowl), sometimes also called *asam 'takra* (the guinea-fowl's feather), and sometimes *Kotwa* (a scar).

44 *Oyokoman Asonawo.* This is a composite design, borrowing something from the *Oyoko* clan cloth (no. 29), and another pattern called *Asonawa*, hence the name.

25

Rattray's silk swatches continued:

45 *Yaa Kete*; called after a princess of that name; it might be worn by any one of the *Oyoko* royal family.

46 *Yaa Atta.* Yaa Atta was a former Queen Mother of Kokofu, in the reign of King Bonsu the Elder (about A D 1800). This cloth was formerly worn only by Queen Mothers of Kokofu, Bekwai, Coomassie, Nsuta, or Mampon.

47 *Apea Akobi*; he was a weaver who lived at Bonwere during the reign of Akusi Bodom (about A D 1750); formerly this design was only worn by the King of Ashanti.

48 *Oyokoman Amponhema*, a slight variation of no. 29. The King of Ashanti's great state umbrella was covered with cloth of this pattern.

49 *Amanahyiamu* ('the nation have met together').

A cloth of this design was worn by the King of Ashanti at the *Odwira* ceremony. The great chiefs might also wear it with the king's permission.

50 *Nwotoa Adweneasa.... Nwotoa* means shuttles, and this design is said to be woven 'with a shuttle in either hand'.

51 *Amponsim* or *Akurase.* Amponsim is a person's name; *akurase* means 'the mouse's tooth'. This design is said to have been first worn by a chief (Adunku) who lived in the reign of Osai Tutu and was the first to fight the famous Ntim Gyakari, before the latter was defeated and slain at Feyiase.

52 *Srafo* (the army on the march).

53 *Asonawo mmada.* The clan 'tartan' of the Asona tribe; the father of King Bonsu Panyin was Owusu Ansa, who belonged to the Asona clan, the first of that clan ever to be the father of an Ashanti king. The pattern is said to have originated in this fact.

54 *Agobamu.* Said to be a personal name; formerly only worn by the Queen Mother of Ashanti.

55 *Yaa Amanpene* ('Yaa whom the nation loves'). Originally called after one of the daughters of King Osai Kojo. The Bonwere weavers say it is one of the *Dokoasiri* patterns.

56 *Akoabena.* Called after the mother of Ntim Gyakari, King of Denkira, who was slain by Osai Tutu.

57 *Dokoasiri fodua.* Said to be another variety of [plate 24] no. 26. The Bonwere weavers call it *Amanpene*; it might be worn by any of the greater *amanhene* (paramount chiefs).

58 *Wirempe ko gyina* ('the Wirempe go to consult together'); worn by the Gyase chief.

59 *Dado* or *Ansaku*. The former word said to be derived from the name of the wife of a weaver who lived in ancient times, called Kuragu Yaa.

60 *Sika futuru* (gold dust); might, in former times, only be worn by the King of Ashanti.

61 *Bewo*, called after a princess of the *Oyoko* clan who married the chief of Tafo during the reign of Osai Tutu.

62 *Gyimikye*, called after the weaver (a native of Bonwere) who designed it.

63 *Nsankani koko* (the yellow Nsankani flower). Formerly worn only by the King and Queen Mother of Ashanti.

64 *Tiafo* ('he who tramples upon'). A sobriquet of the King of Ashanti, and formerly worn only by him. The Bonwere weavers, however, state that the name of this pattern is *onyina ne no man* (the silk-cotton tree and its branches).

65 *Yiwa ne Bota* (the Yiwa and Bota beads). Formerly only worn by the King of Ashanti; the Bonwere weavers say it is one of the *Dokoasiri* designs.

66 *Owireduwa*. Called after a woman of that name (*Owireduwa Akwafu*), who lived in the reign of Osai Kwame (1781); only worn by Queen Mothers.

26

Rattray's silk swatches continued:

67 *Agyapoma*. The favourite wife of King Osai Tutu, who is also reported to have called his favourite gun after her; formerly only worn by the King and Queen Mother.

68 *'Dumrane* (the great *odum* tree); also called *Asonawo tuntum* (the black *Asonawo*, see [plate 25] no. 53). The first name was also a title of the Ashanti kings; formerly only worn by the Kings of Ashanti.

69 *Amma Benewa*. Called after a woman of that name. She is said to have been the sister of a chief called Tibo of Asen (near Cape Coast), where the people of Asen who originally came from Adanse first settled, in the reign of Kwabia Amanfi (A D 1600).

70 *Akyem konmu* (the neck of the Akyem bird); might be worn by any *omanhen'* (paramount chief).

71 *Higya* (the lion); formerly only worn by the King of Ashanti.

72 *Semea*. This is a comparatively modern pattern, said to have been introduced from Kwitta. The warp is composed of black threads, the weft of yellow. No other weft designs are introduced.

73 *Nkwadwe* ('all my subjects are in peace'). The cushions in the King of Ashanti's hammock were made of this pattern.

74 *Amoako ne Asare* (Amoako and Asare). Amoako was the *Ko'ntire hene* to chief Asare of Kokofu.

75 *Atabia tuntum* (the black Atabia), named after a weaver, Atabia, who lived in the reign of King Bonsu II (*circa* A D 1877).

76 *Akyem ntama* (the shield-bearer's cloth), formerly only worn by that body. The Ashanti formerly carried shields and bows and arrows, but so long ago that the shape of the shields is now only known to us in the form of Ashanti weights.

77 *Mmada Asonawo Ahahamono* (the fresh green *mmada Asonawo*); see [plate 25] no. 53.

78 *Panpana ahahan* (Panpana leaves); formerly worn only by the King of Ashanti.

79 *Takyiawo*. Said to be called after a favourite wife of King Kwaku Dua I (A D 1838).

80 *Adwowa Koko* (the red Adwowa). Said to have been the wife of one Pampo, a weaver of Bonwere.

81 *Amankuo*. Said to have been called after a chief of that name (Nti Amoa Amankuo), who was killed by the chief of Juabin in the reign of Osai Tutu.

82 *Aserewa Monom* (the smooth *Aserewa* bird); the Bonwere weavers say it is one of the *Dokoasiri* designs.

83 *Nkotimsefuopua* (the Queen Mother's court officials' tuft); so called from the fashion of dressing the hair (*pua*).

84 *Adwobi*. Said to be called after the wife of a weaver, Kofi Nyame by name. Kofi Nyame is also said to have designed the pattern called *akyempim* (see [plate 24] no. 31). This pattern was formerly only worn by the wives of the Ashanti king.

85 *Kontomponi wafere* ('the liar is put to shame').

86 *Manhyia Ntama* (the meeting of the nation cloth).

87 *'Kontomerie Ahahan* (the tender leaf of the coco-yam). Formerly worn by the King of Ashanti, and also by the chief of Jamasi.

88 *Dwuma Horodo* (young bud of the *Dwuma* tree).

27

Rattray's silk swatches continued:

89 *Emmo* (rice). The King of Ashanti, when 'washing his soul', is said to have worn this pattern.

90 *Dokoasiri Krofa*, one of the *Dokoasiri* patterns, formerly only worn by the *Oyoko* clan.

91 *Konkroma Tenten*. The tall Konkroma tree, but called by the Bonwere weavers *Asebi*.

92 *Kradie* (the Satisfied Soul).

93 *Atta Birago* (Birago, the twin). Birago was a Queen Mother of Kokofu during the reign of King Bonsu Panyin.

94 *Afua Kobi*. Called after the Queen Mother of that name; she was the mother of King Kakari and of King Mensa Bonsu.

95 *Nkontompo ntama* (the liar's cloth). The King of Ashanti is said to have worn this pattern when holding court, to confute persons of doubtful veracity who came before him.

96 *Anwonomoase* (the root of the *anwonomo* plant). Worn only by special permission of the King of Ashanti. This design signifies happiness: 'The *anwomono* root is sweet.'

97 *Bodom Bosuo*. The *Bodom* is the name of a precious bead. The Bonwere weavers call this pattern *Gyimekye*.

98 *Srafo*, see also [plate 25] no. 52.

99 *Asambo*, see also [plate 24] no. 43.

28

Rattray's silk swatches continued:

100 See also [plate 24] no. 42. This is the weft pattern.

101 Showing the weft pattern of [plate 26] no. 80.

102 Showing the weft pattern of [plate 27] no. 91.

29

Rattray's silk swatches continued:

103 Showing the weft of [plate 23] no. 20.
104 Showing the weft of [plate 24] no. 29.
105 Showing the weft of [plate 24] no. 39.

30

Rattray's silk swatches continued:

106–8 Showing the weft of [plate 27] no. 95; [plate 23] no. 3 and no. 14, respectively.

31

Type of cloth Ewe man's cloth
Local title of cloth Adanudo
Origin by tribe/group Ewe-Adangbe
Place of origin Kpetoe, Ghana
Type of yarn Cotton warp and weft
Weaving techniques Plain weave with single and double supplementary wefts
Number of strips 24
Overall size of cloth 169 × 280 cm

This cotton cloth is so tightly woven that the double inlay areas 'pinch' the strips, creating a flowing movement within the composition. Single-weave inlay patterns visible on this cloth include combs, knives, paddles and the crescent moon.

The definition of the cloth as 'Adanudo' refers to its superior quality in terms of painstaking workmanship. Such a cloth would have been commissioned by a wealthy man or woman; the Ashanti equivalent is 'Nsaduaso'.

32

Type of cloth Ewe woman's cloth
Local title of cloth Vidzikpe Adanudo
Origin by tribe/group Ewe-Adangbe
Place of origin Kpetoe, Ghana
Type of yarn Cotton warp and weft
Weaving techniques Plain weave with single and double supplementary wefts
Number of strips 12
Overall size of cloth 90 × 182 cm

There is much confusion over the provenance of this type of cloth; the border work is seen as an Ashanti hallmark, yet the figurative decoration is of the distinctive Ewe style. Such a rigorous *susudua* composition certainly benefits from being broken up by the figurative work. The title of the cloth was given by the chief weaver of Kpetoe as *Vidzikpe*: 'This is the cloth used by our mothers after giving birth to child. They used this cloth, as tradition demands, when going round to thank those who helped them during childbirth.'

33

Type of cloth Ewe man's cloth
Local title of cloth Avonwe
Origin by tribe/group Ewe-Anlo
Place of origin Keta Lagoon area/Agbozume, Ghana
Type of yarn Cotton warp and weft with rayon

supplementary wefts
Weaving techniques Plain weave with double supplementary wefts
Number of strips 20
Overall size of cloth 186 × 301 cm

This cloth represents an intermediary stage between the simple striped cloths of plain weave, and the heavily inlaid Adanudo examples. Here, scattered on the striped ground of an Avonwe cloth, is a dusting of double-weave inlay motifs woven in bright rayon colours.

34

Type of cloth Ewe man's cloth
Local title of cloth Avonwe
Origin by tribe/group Ewe-Anlo
Place of origin Keta Lagoon area, Ghana
Type of yarn Cotton warp and weft
Weaving techniques Plain weave
Number of strips 27
Overall size of cloth 223 × 300 cm

The title of this cloth, which comes from the southern district of the Ewe people, is derived from *avon*, meaning cloth, and *we*, meaning good. Such a wrap, employing a relatively simple construction technique, would be titled 'N'tama' by the Ashanti.

35

Type of cloth Ewe man's cloth
Local title of cloth Adzoa Foli Adanudo

Origin by tribe/group Ewe-Adangbe
Place of origin Kpetoe, Ghana
Type of yarn Cotton warp and weft
Weaving techniques Plain weave with single and double supplementary wefts
Number of strips 21
Overall size of cloth 178 × 300 cm

'*Adzoa Foli*. This cloth is named in memory of the wife of Togbe Foli.'

36

Type of cloth Ewe man's cloth
Local title of cloth Adanudo
Origin by tribe/group Ewe-Adangbe
Place of origin Kpetoe, Ghana
Type of yarn Cotton warp and weft
Weaving techniques Plain weave with single and double supplementary wefts
Number of strips 22
Overall size of cloth 175 × 296 cm

Set against this simple striped background are the first examples of the masterful figurative work and colour associations that are typical of the Ewe Adanudo cloths.

37

Type of cloth Ewe man's cloth
Local title of cloth Wogbloese Adanudo
Origin by tribe/group Ewe-Adangbe
Place of origin Kpetoe, Ghana

Type of yarn Cotton warp and weft
Weaving techniques Plain weave with single and double supplementary wefts
Number of strips 20
Overall size of cloth 175 × 277 cm

'*Wogbloese*: they talk and hear.' The composition of this cloth follows the *susudua* layout, in which evenly spaced inlays sandwich the finely detailed motifs.

38
Detail of plate 37

39
Type of cloth Ewe man's cloth
Local title of cloth Megbenu Adanudo
Origin by tribe/group Ewe-Adangbe
Place of origin Kpetoe, Ghana
Type of yarn Cotton warp and weft
Weaving techniques Plain weave with single and double supplementary wefts
Number of strips 24

'*Megbenu*: back thing.' The length of the inlay patterns is unusual in this cloth; here, motifs, such as hands, have 'escaped' from being bound within the inlay blocks and appear to run with, as well as across the warp.

40
Type of cloth Ewe man's cloth
Local title of cloth Adanudo

Origin by tribe/group Ewe-Adangbe
Place of origin Kpetoe, Ghana
Type of yarn Cotton warp and weft
Weaving techniques Plain weave with single and double supplementary wefts
Number of strips 20
Overall size of cloth 150 × 282 cm

41
(Detail)
Type of cloth Ewe man's cloth
Local title of cloth Fiawoyome Adanudo
Origin by tribe/group Ewe-Adangbe
Place of origin Kpetoe, Ghana
Type of yarn Cotton warp and weft
Weaving techniques Plain weave with single and double supplementary wefts
Number of strips 16
Overall size of cloth 123 × 221 cm

'*Fiawoyome*: behind the chiefs.'

42
(Detail)
Type of cloth Ewe woman's cloth
Local title of cloth Adanudo
Origin by tribe/group Ewe-Adangbe
Place of origin Kpetoe, Ghana
Type of yarn Cotton warp and weft
Weaving techniques Plain weave with single and double supplementary wefts
Number of strips 14

Overall size of cloth 169 × 280 cm

The 'Ashanti'-style border treatment at the fringe is often seen on Ewe women's cloths.

43
(Detail)
Type of cloth Ewe woman's cloth
Local title of cloth Adanudo
Origin by tribe/group Ewe-Adangbe
Place of origin Kpetoe, Ghana
Type of yarn Cotton warp and weft
Weaving techniques Plain weave with single and double supplementary wefts
Number of strips 14
Overall size of cloth 104 × 187 cm

The rigorous grid of blue and white patterning on the warps of this cloth is most demanding on the eye.

44–47
(Details)
Type of cloth Ewe man's cloth
Local title of cloth Adanudo
Origin by tribe/group Ewe-Adangbe
Place of origin Kpetoe, Ghana
Type of yarn Cotton warp and weft
Weaving techniques Plain weave with single and double supplementary wefts

A wide variety of motifs, including scorpions, guinea-fowl, cattle, chickens, snakes, swords and people, float

within and without the inlay blocks on this finely worked cloth.

48
(Detail)
Type of cloth Ewe man's cloth
Local title of cloth Adanudo
Origin by tribe/group Ewe-Adangbe
Place of origin Kpetoe, Ghana
Type of yarn Cotton warp and weft
Weaving techniques Warp float weave with single and double supplementary wefts
Number of strips 23
Overall size of cloth 167 × 300 cm

As a result of the painstaking weaving technique employed in this example, when one looks at the back of the cloth (plate 49) the contrasting warp colours are revealed.

49
Verso of plate 48; detail

50
(Detail)
Type of cloth Ewe man's cloth
Local title of cloth Adanudo
Origin by tribe/group Ewe-Adangbe
Place of origin Kpetoe, Ghana
Type of yarn Cotton warp and weft
Weaving techniques Plain weave with single and double supplementary wefts

Number of strips 24
Overall size of cloth 200 × 300 cm

The very 'tight' *susudua* composition of the inlay blocks is combined with an ingenious warp stripe pattern to make this cloth shimmer with shades of gold, red and blue.

51

Type of cloth Ewe man's cloth
Local title of cloth Adanudo
Origin by tribe/group Ewe-Adangbe
Place of origin Kpetoe, Ghana
Type of yarn Cotton warp and weft
Weaving techniques Plain weave with single and double supplementary wefts
Number of strips 19
Overall size of cloth 160 × 282 cm

The 'error' within the central area of this old cloth is more than likely associated with damage and repair; the remaining strips have been linked together as effectively as possible.

Crustacea and cutlery, hands and pots are just some of the many motifs to be found on this richly patterned cloth.

52

Type of cloth Ewe man's cloth
Local title of cloth Adanudo
Origin by tribe/group Ewe-Adangbe
Place of origin Kpetoe, Ghana

Type of yarn Cotton warp and weft
Weaving techniques Plain weave with single and double supplementary wefts
Number of strips 21
Overall size of cloth 168 × 261 cm

The thoughtful arrangement of yellow, orange and red inlay blocks makes this *susudua* composition seem, at first glance, to be out of synchronization, though it creates a harmonious whole.

53

Type of cloth Ewe woman's cloth
Local title of cloth Adanudo
Origin by tribe/group Ewe-Adangbe
Place of origin Kpetoe, Ghana
Type of yarn Cotton warp and weft
Weaving techniques Plain weave with single and double supplementary wefts
Number of strips 13
Overall size of cloth 94 × 150 cm

This woman's textile has most probably been cut down from a larger damaged man's cloth.

54

Detail of plate 56

55

Type of cloth Ewe woman's cloth
Local title of cloth Adanudo
Origin by tribe/group Ewe-Adangbe

Place of origin Kpetoe, Ghana
Type of yarn Cotton warp and weft
Weaving techniques Plain weave with single and double supplementary wefts
Number of strips 14
Overall size of cloth 117 × 202 cm

56

Type of cloth Ewe man's cloth
Local title of cloth Adanudo
Origin by tribe/group Ewe-Adangbe
Place of origin Kpetoe, Ghana
Type of yarn Cotton warp and weft
Weaving techniques Plain weave with single and double supplementary wefts
Number of strips 20
Overall size of cloth 178 × 305 cm

Yellow inlay blocks break up this lattice of *susudua* to great effect.

57

Type of cloth Ewe woman's cloth
Local title of cloth Degato Adanudo
Origin by tribe/group Ewe-Adangbe
Place of origin Kpetoe, Ghana
Type of yarn Cotton warp and weft
Weaving techniques Plain weave with single and double supplementary wefts
Number of strips 14
Overall size of cloth 98 × 186 cm

'*Degato*: there is a new invention.' This may, perhaps, refer to the most unusual warp stripe colour combination.

58

Type of cloth Ewe woman's cloth
Local title of cloth Nyehameva Adanudo
Origin by tribe/group Ewe-Adangbe
Place of origin Kpetoe, Ghana
Type of yarn Cotton warp and weft
Weaving techniques Plain weave with single and double supplementary wefts
Number of strips 13
Overall size of cloth 122 × 214 cm

'*Nyehameva*: I have also come.' The use of inlay weft bars, at first positioned to form a boundary to the motifs, extends in this cloth to their abstract placement within the field – a design technique demonstrated by the cloths at the end of the colour section of this book (plates 74–80). The lack of continuity in the composition is the result of repair to the cloth.

59

Type of cloth Ewe woman's cloth
Local title of cloth Atsusikpodzedzome Adanudo
Origin by tribe/group Ewe-Adangbe
Place of origin Kpetoe, Ghana
Type of yarn Cotton warp and weft
Weaving techniques Plain weave with single and double supplementary wefts

Number of strips 13
Overall size of cloth 113 × 185 cm

'*Atsusikpodzedzome*: this cloth was presented by a husband to one of the rival wives. The other wife was so disturbed that she fell into the fire on seeing the cloth presented to her rival.'

60

Type of cloth Ewe man's cloth
Local title of cloth Gbete Adanudo
Origin by tribe/group Ewe-Adangbe
Place of origin Kpetoe, Ghana
Type of yarn Cotton warp and weft
Weaving techniques Plain weave with single and double supplementary wefts
Number of strips 20
Overall size of cloth 158 × 288 cm

'*Gbete*: a name of a fetish.'

61

(Detail)
Type of cloth Ewe man's cloth
Local title of cloth Adanudo
Origin by tribe/group Ewe-Adangbe
Place of origin Kpetoe, Ghana
Type of yarn Cotton warp and weft
Weaving techniques Plain weave with single and double supplementary wefts
Number of strips 18
Overall size of cloth 150 × 282 cm

62

Type of cloth Ewe woman's cloth
Local title of cloth Adanudo
Origin by tribe/group Ewe-Adangbe
Place of origin Kpetoe, Ghana
Type of yarn Cotton warp and weft
Weaving techniques Plain weave with single and double supplementary wefts
Number of strips 14
Overall size of cloth 110 × 170 cm

This cloth is noteworthy for the use of a 'selvedge' strip, complete with weft bars but no pattern blocks.

63

Type of cloth Ewe woman's cloth
Local title of cloth Adanudo
Origin by tribe/group Ewe-Adangbe
Place of origin Kpetoe, Ghana
Type of yarn Cotton warp and weft
Weaving techniques Plain weave with single and double supplementary wefts
Number of strips 14
Overall size of cloth 114 × 181 cm

64

Type of cloth Ewe man's cloth
Local title of cloth Adanudo
Origin by tribe/group Ewe-Adangbe
Place of origin Kpetoe, Ghana
Type of yarn Cotton warp and weft
Weaving techniques Plain weave with single and

double supplementary wefts
Number of strips 22
Overall size of cloth 176 × 282 cm

The single supplementary weft work includes the appearance of a group of figures, most probably a chief and his advisers with their staffs of office at a durbar.

65

Detail of plate 64

66

Type of cloth Ewe man's cloth(?)
Local title of cloth Adanudo
Origin by tribe/group Ewe-Adangbe
Place of origin Kpetoe, Ghana
Type of yarn Cotton warp and weft
Weaving techniques Plain weave with single and double supplementary wefts
Number of strips 20
Overall size of cloth 160 × 250 cm

67

Type of cloth Ewe man's cloth
Local title of cloth Adanudo
Origin by tribe/group Ewe-Adangbe
Place of origin Kpetoe, Ghana
Type of yarn Cotton warp and weft
Weaving techniques Plain weave with single and double supplementary wefts
Number of strips 21
Overall size of cloth 152 × 276 cm

An old cloth much damaged and repaired by the cutting and moving of strips.

68

Type of cloth Ewe man's cloth
Local title of cloth Adanudo
Origin by tribe/group Ewe-Adangbe
Place of origin Kpetoe, Ghana
Type of yarn Cotton warp and weft
Weaving techniques Plain weave with single and double supplementary wefts
Number of strips 20
Overall size of cloth 172 × 300 cm

Although it seems quite plain, evenly made and simple, this cloth is nevertheless packed with figurative work.

69

Detail of plate 68

70

(Detail)
Type of cloth Ewe man's cloth
Local title of cloth Gebekor Adanudo
Origin by tribe/group Ewe-Adangbe
Place of origin Kpetoe, Ghana
Type of yarn Cotton warp and weft
Weaving techniques Plain weave with single and double supplementary wefts
Number of strips 22
Overall size of cloth 171 × 290 cm

The title *Gebekor* refers to the name of a traditional drum. The Ewe are well known, not only for their powers of ju-ju, but also for their prowess at drumming. The multitude of weft bars in this cloth breaks up the widely spaced inlay blocks with great success.

71

Type of cloth Ewe man's cloth
Local title of cloth Adanudo
Origin by tribe/group Ewe-Adangbe
Place of origin Kpetoe, Ghana
Type of yarn Cotton warp and weft
Weaving techniques Plain weave with single and double supplementary wefts
Number of strips 20
Overall size of cloth 172 × 274 cm

The tiny figurative designs within the inlay blocks are an unusual feature of this cloth.

72

Type of cloth Ewe man's cloth
Local title of cloth Adanudo
Origin by tribe/group Ewe-Adangbe
Place of origin Kpetoe, Ghana
Type of yarn Cotton warp and weft
Weaving techniques Plain weave with single and double supplementary wefts
Number of strips 22
Overall size of cloth 174 × 293 cm

In this elegant cloth, some of the figurative designs form the inlay blocks as well as appearing freely within the field.

73–76

Details of plate 72

77

Type of cloth Ewe man's cloth
Local title of cloth Adanudo
Origin by tribe/group Ewe-Adangbe
Place of origin Kpetoe, Ghana
Type of yarn Cotton warp and weft
Weaving techniques Plain weave with single and double supplementary wefts
Number of strips 24
Overall size of cloth 175 × 277 cm

This is the more regular of the two lattice-type compositions illustrated here (see plate 78).

78

Type of cloth Ewe man's cloth
Local title of cloth Adanudo
Origin by tribe/group Ewe-Adangbe
Place of origin Kpetoe, Ghana
Type of yarn Cotton warp and weft
Weaving techniques Plain weave with single and double supplementary wefts
Number of strips 18
Overall size of cloth 156 × 275 cm

79
Type of cloth Ewe man's cloth
Local title of cloth Adanudo
Origin by tribe/group Ewe-Adangbe
Place of origin Kpetoe, Ghana
Type of yarn Cotton warp and weft
Weaving techniques Plain weave with single and double supplementary wefts
Number of strips 23
Overall size of cloth 192 × 298 cm

The background wefts of this cloth form a 'web' that adds an extra dimension to the patterning.

80 *(Detail)*
Type of cloth Ewe woman's cloth
Local title of cloth Adanudo
Origin by tribe/group Ewe-Adangbe
Place of origin Kpetoe, Ghana
Type of yarn Cotton warp and weft
Weaving techniques Plain weave with single and double supplementary wefts
Number of strips 13
Overall size of cloth 112 × 180 cm

The one mis-matching strip is a discordant element in this otherwise perfect cloth.

81 *(Detail)*
Type of cloth Ewe man's cloth
Local title of cloth Susuavor Adanudo
Origin by tribe/group Ewe-Adangbe

Place of origin Kpetoe, Ghana
Type of yarn Cotton warp and weft
Weaving techniques Plain weave with single and double supplementary wefts
Number of strips 21
Overall size of cloth 180 × 280 cm

The *Susuavor* or *Susuvu* title for Ewe cloths is the equivalent to the Ashanti *Adweneasa* ('my skills are exhausted', or 'all patterns have come to an end'), denoting that all possible artifice and skill have been used to pattern the cloth with supplementary designs.

82
Type of cloth Ewe man's cloth
Local title of cloth Asasa Adanudo
Origin by tribe/group Ewe-Adangbe
Place of origin Kpetoe, Ghana
Type of yarn Cotton warp and weft
Weaving techniques Plain weave with single and double supplementary wefts
Number of strips 17
Overall size of cloth 150 × 250 cm

This cloth is most probably missing at least three of its strips as a result of damage or staining. Their removal has transformed this textile into an 'Asasa', or mixed example (Mmaban in Ashanti terms).

83
Type of cloth Ewe man's cloth(?)
Local title of cloth Adanudo

Origin by tribe/group Ewe-Adangbe
Place of origin Kpetoe, Ghana
Type of yarn Cotton warp and weft
Weaving techniques Plain weave with single and double supplementary wefts
Number of strips 17
Overall size of cloth 162 × 248 cm

This is a curiously 'in-between' size of cloth, in terms of both its dimensions and the number of strips. As in the case of the cloths that follow, this Ewe wrap shows the familiar less decorated 'selvedge' strips, together with an extensive use of inlay weft bars and a 'waisting' to the cloth.

84

Type of cloth Ewe man's cloth
Local title of cloth Anyahu Adanudo
Origin by tribe/group Ewe-Adangbe
Place of origin Kpetoe, Ghana
Type of yarn Cotton warp and weft
Weaving techniques Plain weave with single and double supplementary wefts
Number of strips 22
Overall size of cloth 176 × 306 cm

Although composed of two different patterns of warp stripes, this cloth is not of the Asasa variety, for here is a regular and complete composition, well balanced by the use of twinned warp stripes. There is no doubt, however, that no matter how successful this concept is to Western eyes, the Ewe and Ashanti weavers and

their clients view 'mixed' cloths of any description as inferior in value to the 'pure' textiles.

85

Type of cloth Ewe man's cloth
Local title of cloth Adanudo
Origin by tribe/group Ewe-Adangbe
Place of origin Kpetoe, Ghana
Type of yarn Cotton warp and weft
Weaving techniques Plain weave with single and double supplementary wefts
Number of strips 16
Overall size of cloth 140 × 293 cm

This cloth is patterned in the Susuavor style.

86

(Detail)
Type of cloth Ewe woman's cloth
Local title of cloth Adanudo
Origin by tribe/group Ewe-Adangbe
Place of origin Kpetoe, Ghana
Type of yarn Cotton warp and weft
Weaving techniques Plain weave with single and double supplementary wefts
Number of strips 14
Overall size of cloth 101 × 190 cm

The single colour inlay blocks of this cloth betray their unusual 'tweed-like' weaving origins. Through the plying together of differing colours of warp threads, a 'speckled' effect is achieved.

87

(Detail)

Type of cloth Ewe man's cloth
Local title of cloth Adanudo
Origin by tribe/group Ewe-Adangbe
Place of origin Kpetoe, Ghana
Type of yarn Cotton warp and weft
Weaving techniques Plain weave with single and
double supplementary wefts
Number of strips 21
Overall size of cloth 189 × 297 cm

The single supplementary decorative wefts have
'escaped' from within the inlay blocks, so that the
various motifs – calabashes, people and birds – appear
to 'move' out of the overall pattern of the cloth.

88

(Detail)

Type of cloth Ewe man's cloth
Local title of cloth Agbefeavi Adanudo
Origin by tribe/group Ewe-Adangbe
Place of origin Kpetoe, Ghana
Type of yarn Cotton warp and weft
Weaving techniques Plain weave with single and
double supplementary wefts
Number of strips 19
Overall size of cloth 194 × 275 cm

The title of the cloth, *Agbefeavi*, translates as 'we must
cry for long life'.

89

Type of cloth Ewe man's cloth
Local title of cloth Gbofoteme Susuavor Adanudo
Origin by tribe/group Ewe-Adangbe
Place of origin Kpetoe, Ghana
Type of yarn Cotton warp and weft
Weaving techniques Plain weave with single and
double supplementary wefts
Number of strips 21
Overall size of cloth 165 × 306 cm

The full title of this cloth is *Gbofoteme Norvi
Susuavor*, and the description given by an Ewe weaver
reads: 'The background design is *Gbofoteme*. The
symbolic meaning is that several designs and art came
into play to make this cloth. The designers concluded
that it was a masterpiece.'

90

Type of cloth Ewe man's cloth
Local title of cloth Susuavor Adanudo
Origin by tribe/group Ewe-Adangbe
Place of origin Kpetoe, Ghana
Type of yarn Cotton warp and weft
Weaving techniques Plain weave with single and
double supplementary wefts
Number of strips 17
Overall size of cloth 126 × 237 cm

A cloth signed by its maker.

91
Type of cloth Ewe man's cloth
Local title of cloth Susuavor Adanudo
Origin by tribe/group Ewe-Adangbe
Place of origin Kpetoe, Ghana
Type of yarn Cotton warp and weft
Weaving techniques Plain weave with single and
double supplementary wefts
Number of strips 22
Overall size of cloth 171 × 260 cm

This cloth opens a section of colour plates devoted to
Susuavor textiles. Here the weaver has exhausted the
possibilities for further weft decoration, packing the
cloth with inanimate and animate motifs.

92
Type of cloth Ewe man's cloth
Local title of cloth Susuavor Adanudo
Origin by tribe/group Ewe-Adangbe
Place of origin Kpetoe, Ghana
Type of yarn Cotton warp and weft
Weaving techniques Plain weave with single and
double supplementary wefts
Number of strips 19

The few blocks left undecorated within this cloth
serve to emphasize its dynamic range of inlay
patterning.

93
Type of cloth Ewe man's cloth
Local title of cloth Susuavor Adanudo
Origin by tribe/group Ewe-Adangbe
Place of origin Kpetoe, Ghana
Type of yarn Cotton warp and weft
Weaving techniques Plain weave with single and
double supplementary wefts
Number of strips 20
Overall size of cloth 157 × 274 cm

An electric combination of warp striping and weft
patterning.

94 *(Detail)*
Type of cloth Ewe man's cloth
Local title of cloth Gbesike Susuavor Adanudo
Origin by tribe/group Ewe-Adangbe
Place of origin Kpetoe, Ghana
Type of yarn Cotton warp and weft
Weaving techniques Plain weave with single and
double supplementary wefts
Number of strips 22
Overall size of cloth 190 × 309 cm

'*Gbesike Susuavor*: this is a special design which
denotes that all design and art came into play.' A cloth
that challenges the viewer with its constant matching
and mis-matching of inlay block designs and spacing.
Of the few animate motifs within this textile, the
horse and rider design (below left) is especially
imaginative.

95

Type of cloth Ewe man's cloth
Local title of cloth Susuavor Adanudo
Origin by tribe/group Ewe-Adangbe
Place of origin Kpetoe, Ghana
Type of yarn Cotton warp and weft
Weaving techniques Plain weave with single and double supplementary wefts
Number of strips 19
Overall size of cloth 156 × 286 cm

96

Type of cloth Ewe woman's cloth
Local title of cloth Atifofoe Susuavor Adanudo
Origin by tribe/group Ewe-Adangbe
Place of origin Kpetoe, Ghana
Type of yarn Cotton warp and weft
Weaving techniques Plain weave with single and double supplementary wefts
Number of strips 14

'*Atifofoe Susuavor*: this means that several designs and much skill were needed to make this cloth, so it is considered a masterpiece. This cloth can be made in a different colour background to suit taste.'

97

Type of cloth Ewe woman's cloth
Local title of cloth Susuavor Adanudo
Origin by tribe/group Ewe-Adangbe
Place of origin Kpetoe, Ghana
Type of yarn Cotton warp and weft

Weaving techniques Plain weave with single and double supplementary wefts
Number of strips 13
Overall size of cloth 92 × 183 cm

98

Type of cloth Ewe woman's cloth
Local title of cloth Susuavor Adanudo
Origin by tribe/group Ewe-Adangbe
Place of origin Kpetoe, Ghana
Type of yarn Cotton warp and weft
Weaving techniques Plain weave with single and double supplementary wefts
Number of strips 14
Overall size of cloth 113 × 190 cm

99

Type of cloth Ewe woman's cloth
Local title of cloth Atifofoe Susuavor Adanudo
Origin by tribe/group Ewe-Adangbe
Place of origin Kpetoe, Ghana
Type of yarn Cotton warp and weft
Weaving techniques Plain weave with single and double supplementary wefts
Number of strips 13
Overall size of cloth 122 × 175 cm

100

Type of cloth Ewe man's cloth
Local title of cloth Susuavor Adanudo
Origin by tribe/group Ewe-Adangbe
Place of origin Kpetoe, Ghana

Type of yarn Cotton warp and weft
Weaving techniques Plain weave with single and
double supplementary wefts
Number of strips 22
Overall size of cloth 168 × 304 cm

The lurid colours of the yarn used in the inlay
patterns are a suitable match for the imaginative use
of motifs and letters found within this cloth.

101–102
Details of plate 100

103
Type of cloth Ewe man's cloth
Local title of cloth Susuavor Adanudo
Origin by tribe/group Ewe-Adangbe
Place of origin Kpetoe, Ghana
Type of yarn Cotton warp and weft
Weaving techniques Plain weave with single and
double supplementary wefts
Number of strips 22
Overall size of cloth 185 × 302 cm

An old and well-used cloth.

104
Type of cloth Ewe woman's cloth
Local title of cloth Atrikpoe Asasa Adanudo
Origin by tribe/group Ewe-Adangbe
Place of origin Kpetoe, Ghana
Type of yarn Cotton warp and weft

Weaving techniques Plain weave with single and
double supplementary wefts
Number of strips 11
Overall size of cloth 93 × 149 cm

'*Atrikpoe*. Name of a traditional drum.' At top left,
an upside-down soldier with his tin hat and gun is
visible.

105
Type of cloth Ewe woman's cloth
Local title of cloth Asasa Adanudo
Origin by tribe/group Ewe-Adangbe
Place of origin Kpetoe, Ghana
Type of yarn Cotton warp and weft
Weaving techniques Plain weave with single and
double supplementary wefts
Number of strips 13
Overall size of cloth 121 × 184 cm

This cloth opens a section of colour plates devoted to
mixed cloths that are dynamic and unstable in
composition and therefore full of movement.

106
Type of cloth Ewe woman's cloth
Local title of cloth Asasa Adanudo
Origin by tribe/group Ewe-Adangbe
Place of origin Kpetoe, Ghana
Type of yarn Cotton warp and weft
Weaving techniques Plain weave with single and
double supplementary wefts

Number of strips 10
Overall size of cloth 72 × 176 cm

Despite the missing strips, this cloth is still full of interesting motifs, such as chiefs' stools, hearts and abstract forms.

107

Type of cloth Ewe man's cloth
Local title of cloth Asasa Adanudo
Origin by tribe/group Ewe-Adangbe
Place of origin Kpetoe, Ghana
Type of yarn Cotton warp and weft
Weaving techniques Plain weave with single and double supplementary wefts
Number of strips 21
Overall size of cloth 169 × 300 cm

The most mixed Asasa cloth illustrated here: a truly successful jumble of strips.

108

Type of cloth Ewe man's cloth
Local title of cloth Adanudo
Origin by tribe/group Ewe-Adangbe
Place of origin Kpetoe, Ghana
Type of yarn Cotton warp and weft
Weaving techniques Plain weave with single and double supplementary wefts
Number of strips 20
Overall size of cloth 150 × 267 cm

The writing on this cloth reveals its cost as 'four pounds, ten shillings'. The majority of the rows have, unusually, the same motifs on each strip, such as hearts, combs, chiefs' stools and knives. There is much use of the 'tweeding' of the warps in the plain-coloured inlay blocks (see plate 86).

109

Type of cloth Ewe man's cloth
Local title of cloth Adanudo
Origin by tribe/group Ewe-Adangbe
Place of origin Kpetoe, Ghana
Type of yarn Cotton warp and weft
Weaving techniques Plain weave with single and double supplementary wefts
Number of strips 19
Overall size of cloth 132 × 252 cm

The missing strips have disturbed the composition of this cloth. This textile opens a section of colour plates showing cloths with elongated pattern blocks without figurative work.

110

Type of cloth Ewe man's cloth
Local title of cloth Fiadufe Adanudo
Origin by tribe/group Ewe-Adangbe
Place of origin Kpetoe, Ghana
Type of yarn Cotton warp and weft
Weaving techniques Plain weave with single and double supplementary wefts
Number of strips 20

Overall size of cloth 170 × 276 cm

Fiadufe means kingdom.

111

Type of cloth Ewe woman's cloth
Local title of cloth Adanudo
Origin by tribe/group Ewe-Adangbe
Place of origin Kpetoe, Ghana
Type of yarn Cotton warp and weft
Weaving techniques Plain weave with single and double supplementary wefts
Number of strips 13
Overall size of cloth 100 × 178 cm

An old cloth that has been much patched up, thus disturbing its composition.

112

Type of cloth Ewe woman's cloth
Local title of cloth Adanudo
Origin by tribe/group Ewe-Adangbe
Place of origin Kpetoe, Ghana
Type of yarn Cotton warp and weft
Weaving techniques Plain weave with single and double supplementary wefts
Number of strips 16
Overall size of cloth 103 × 192 cm

113

Type of cloth Ewe man's cloth
Local title of cloth Adanudo
Origin by tribe/group Anlo or Ewe-Adangbe

Place of origin Kpetoe, Ghana
Type of yarn Cotton warp and weft
Weaving techniques Plain weave with single and double supplementary wefts
Number of strips 22
Overall size of cloth 190 × 296 cm

A cloth of simple construction that may have been made in the Ewe-Anlo region of south-eastern Ghana.

114

Type of cloth Ewe man's cloth
Local title of cloth Adanudo
Origin by tribe/group Anlo or Ewe-Adangbe
Place of origin Kpetoe, Ghana
Type of yarn Cotton warp and weft
Weaving techniques Plain weave with single and double supplementary wefts
Number of strips 19
Overall size of cloth 171 × 304 cm

115

Type of cloth Ewe woman's cloth
Local title of cloth Atitsoe-Atitrala Adanudo
Origin by tribe/group Ewe-Adangbe
Place of origin Kpetoe, Ghana
Type of yarn Cotton warp and weft
Weaving techniques Plain weave with single and double supplementary wefts
Number of strips 14
Overall size of cloth 118 × 192 cm

'*Atitsoe-Atitrala*: small stick and long stick.'

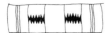

116

Type of cloth Ewe woman's cloth
Local title of cloth Asasa Adanudo
Origin by tribe/group Ewe-Adangbe
Place of origin Kpetoe, Ghana
Type of yarn Cotton warp and weft
Weaving techniques Plain weave with single and double supplementary wefts
Number of strips 14
Overall size of cloth 124 × 187 cm

117

Type of cloth Ewe woman's cloth
Local title of cloth Adanudo
Origin by tribe/group Ewe-Adangbe
Place of origin Kpetoe, Ghana
Type of yarn Cotton warp and weft
Weaving techniques Plain weave with single and double supplementary wefts
Number of strips 14
Overall size of cloth 128 × 180 cm

The 'tweed' inlay blocks so favoured by women clients are clearly seen in this cloth.

118

Type of cloth Ewe man's cloth
Local title of cloth Megbenyezualea Susuavor Adanudo
Origin by tribe/group Ewe-Adangbe
Place of origin Kpetoe, Ghana
Type of yarn Cotton warp and weft
Weaving techniques Plain weave with single and double supplementary wefts
Number of strips 22

'*Megbenyezualea*: my absence becomes a shame.' This cloth shares with plate 130 the distinction of representing the ultimate expression in the combination of Susuavor inlay work, a *susudua* pattern and background warp striping.

119–120

Details of plate 121

121

Type of cloth Ewe man's cloth
Local title of cloth Adanudo
Origin by tribe/group Ewe-Adangbe
Place of origin Kpetoe, Ghana
Type of yarn Cotton warp and weft
Weaving techniques Plain weave with single and double supplementary wefts
Number of strips 24
Overall size of cloth 194 × 327 cm

122

Type of cloth Ewe woman's cloth
Local title of cloth Susuavor Adanudo
Origin by tribe/group Ewe-Adangbe
Place of origin Kpetoe, Ghana
Type of yarn Cotton warp and weft
Weaving techniques Plain weave with single and double supplementary wefts
Number of strips 12

123

Type of cloth Ewe man's cloth
Local title of cloth Gbesike Susuavor Adanudo
Origin by tribe/group Ewe-Adangbe
Place of origin Kpetoe, Ghana
Type of yarn Cotton warp and weft
Weaving techniques Plain weave with single and double supplementary wefts
Number of strips 18
Overall size of cloth 167 × 260 cm

'*Gbesike Susuavor*: this is a special design which denotes that all design and art came into play.'

124

Type of cloth Ewe man's cloth
Local title of cloth Adanudo
Origin by tribe/group Ewe-Adangbe
Place of origin Kpetoe, Ghana
Type of yarn Cotton warp and weft
Weaving techniques Plain weave with single and double supplementary wefts
Number of strips 19
Overall size of cloth 170 × 275 cm

The central composition of clustered motifs is highly unusual.

125

Type of cloth Ewe man's cloth
Local title of cloth Adzida Susuavor Adanudo
Origin by tribe/group Ewe-Adangbe
Place of origin Kpetoe, Ghana
Type of yarn Cotton warp and weft
Weaving techniques Plain weave with single and double supplementary wefts
Number of strips 20
Overall size of cloth 137 × 269 cm

'*Adzida*: name of a traditional drum.'

126

Type of cloth Ewe man's cloth
Local title of cloth Adanudo
Origin by tribe/group Ewe-Adangbe
Place of origin Kpetoe, Ghana
Type of yarn Cotton warp and weft
Weaving techniques Plain weave with single and double supplementary wefts
Number of strips 19

These three cloths all show an abstract use of weft bars within the composition. (See also plate 131.)

127

Type of cloth Ewe man's cloth
Local title of cloth Susuavor Adanudo
Origin by tribe/group Ewe-Adangbe
Place of origin Kpetoe, Ghana
Type of yarn Cotton warp and weft
Weaving techniques Plain weave with single and double supplementary wefts
Number of strips 20
Overall size of cloth 182 × 259 cm

128–129
Details of plate 130

130
Type of cloth Ewe man's cloth
Local title of cloth Susuavor Adanudo
Origin by tribe/group Ewe-Adangbe
Place of origin Kpetoe, Ghana
Type of yarn Cotton warp and weft
Weaving techniques Plain weave with single and
double supplementary wefts
Number of strips 22
Overall size of cloth 176 × 284 cm

This cloth, with its superlative white stripe on a blue
background, combines Susuavor inlay work, a *susudua*

pattern and background warp striping with superb
results. (See also plate 118.)

131
Type of cloth Ewe man's cloth
Local title of cloth Adanudo
Origin by tribe/group Ewe-Adangbe
Place of origin Kpetoe, Ghana
Type of yarn Cotton warp and weft
Weaving techniques Plain weave with single and
double supplementary wefts
Number of strips 19
Overall size of cloth 180 × 270 cm

Unusual offset designs of hens and chiefs' stools can be
found to one end of the cloth.

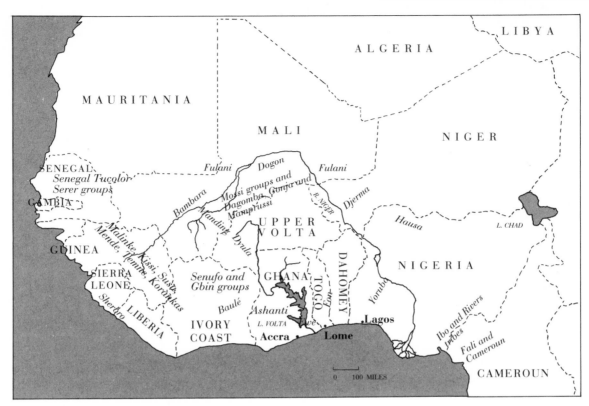

West Africa, political boundaries and weaving groups

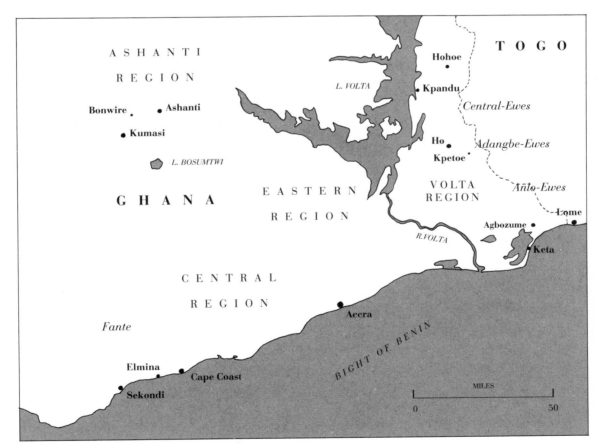

Ashanti and Ewe areas

ILLUSTRATIONS IN THE TEXT
FURTHER READING

Barnard, N., *Living with Decorative Textiles*, 1989

Barnard, N., and J. Gillow, *Traditional Indian Textiles*, 1991

Barth, H., *Travels in North and Central Africa*, 1857–8

Bowdich, T. E., *Mission from Cape Coast Castle to Ashantee*, 1819 (reprinted 1966)

Cole, H. M., and D. H. Ross, *The Arts of Ghana*, 1977

Coombs, D., *The Gold Coast, Britain and the Netherlands: 1850–74*, 1963

Fynn, J. K., *Asante and its Neighbors: 1700–1807*, 1971

Gilfoy, P. S., *Patterns of Life*, 1987

Ibn Battuta, trans. and ed. H. A. R. Gibb, *Travels in Asia and Africa*, 1929

Idiens, D., and K. G. Ponting, eds., *Textiles of Africa*, 1980

Lamb, V., *West African Weaving*, 1975

Lamb, V., and A. Lamb, *The Lamb Collection of West African Narrow Strip Weaving*, 1975

McLoed, M. D., *The Asante*, 1981

Menzel, B., *Textiles of West Africa*, 1972–3

National Museum of Ghana Handbook, 1973

Park, M., *Travels in the Interior Districts of Africa*, 1799

Picton, J., and J. Mack, *African Textiles*, 1989

Rattray, R. S., *Ashanti*, 1923; *Religion and Art in Ashanti*, 1927; *Akan-Ashanti Folk Tales*, 1930

Ross, D. H., and T. F. Garrard, eds., *Akan Transformations*, 1983

Sieber, R., *African Textiles and Decorative Arts*, 1972

Trowell, K. M., *African Design*, 1960

Vlach, J. M., *The Afro-American Tradition in Decorative Arts*, 1978

GLOSSARY

Adanudo High-quality Ewe cloth woven primarily for wealthy chiefs and elders. Usually of high-grade cotton, it is intricately patterned with rich blocks of colour containing single and double inlay motifs.

Ahwepan Ashanti term for cotton or silk cloth patterned with simple warp stripes.

asanan Second set of heddles on a drag loom, used to create inlay designs.

Asasia Ashanti term for silk cloths reserved exclusively for royalty and their attendants, characterized by complex twill inlay patterns.

asatia First set of heddles on a loom, carrying the background weave.

babadua Colour inlays in Ashanti silk cloths.

bankuo Inlaid blocks of solid colour in Ashanti cotton cloths.

dadabena Used to wind the skeins of yarn from the *fwiridie* onto the bobbins (*dodowa*).

dodowa Bobbins that hold the yarn for the weft and weft inlays.

Faprenu Fine-quality silk cloths with complex inlay patterns worked in a double-weave technique.

fwiridie Four-armed, rotating weft skein winder.

hanbels Flat-woven wearing blankets from Morocco, patterned with narrow stripes. Modern term for *lamben*.

khasa Wool or wool-and-cotton textiles, woven by the Fulani nomads of the Niger river bend area, which enjoyed a special status among the Ashanti and other Akan tribes.

kurokurowa Shuttles containing the bobbins that are wound with coloured yarn for the weft.

kyekye 'From afar': cotton strip-woven cloth from the Bondoukou area of the Ivory Coast, simply patterned with stripes or checks in blue and undyed white.

kyereye Beater or comb used to tamp down the weft threads evenly.

lambens North African wearing cloths popular with the Ashanti.

menokomenam 'I walk alone': bobbin-carrier used for laying the warp threads.

Mmaban 'Mixed': cotton or silk cloths made from strips left over from other cloths.

Nsa Cloth of camel's hair and wool, woven by the Fulani weavers of the Savannah.

Nsaduaso High quality silk cloths that do not employ the taboo techniques and twill inlay patterns of Ashanti Asasia production.

N'tama Ashanti term for any type of cloth that is not Asasia, ranging from cotton cloths for the use of the 'common' classes to high quality silk work for nobles, merchants and chiefs.

susudua The even and alternate spacing of blocks of pattern and colour to create a regular chequerboard effect across the whole cloth. Also refers to the measuring stick used to create such patterns successfully.

tabon Swordstick used for the insertion of weft inlay patterns.

Topreko Ashanti cloth, generally of silk, employing simple weft inlays.

INDEX